Immigrant Women
in the Settlement of Missouri

D0062518

PROJECT SPONSORS

Missouri Center for the Book

Western Historical Manuscript Collection,
University of Missouri–Columbia

SPECIAL THANKS

Christine Montgomery, State Historical
Society of Missouri, Columbia

Claudia Powell, Western Historical Manuscript
Collection, University of Missouri–Columbia

MISSOURI HERITAGE READERS
General Editor, Rebecca B. Schroeder

Each Missouri Heritage Reader explores a particular aspect of the state's rich cultural heritage. Focusing on people, places, historical events, and the details of daily life, these books illustrate the ways in which people from all parts of the world contributed to the development of the state and the region. The books incorporate documentary and oral history, folklore, and informal literature in a way that makes these resources accessible to all Missourians.

Intended primarily for adult new readers, these books will also be invaluable to readers of all ages interested in the cultural and social history of Missouri.

OTHER BOOKS IN THE SERIES

Arrow Rock: The Story of a Missouri Village, by Authorene Wilson Phillips

Blind Boone: Missouri's Ragtime Pioneer, by Jack A. Batterson

Called to Courage: Four Women in Missouri History, by Margot Ford McMillen and Heather Roberson

Catfish, Fiddles, Mules, and More: Missouri's State Symbols, by John C. Fisher

Food in Missouri: A Cultural Stew, by Madeline Matson

George Caleb Bingham: Missouri's Famed Painter and Forgotten Politician, Paul C. Nagel

German Settlement in Missouri: New Land, Old Ways, by Robyn K. Burnett and Ken Luebbering

Hoecakes, Hambone, and All That Jazz: African American Traditions in Missouri, by Rose M. Nolen

Into the Spotlight: Four Missouri Women, by Margot Ford McMillen and Heather Roberson

Jane Froman: Missouri's First Lady of Song, by Ilene Stone

Jesse James and the Civil War in Missouri, by Robert L. Dyer

Missouri at Sea: Warships with Show-Me State Names, by Richard E. Schroeder

On Shaky Ground: The New Madrid Earthquakes of 1811–1812, by Norma Hayes Bagnall

Orphan Trains to Missouri, by Michael D. Patrick and Evelyn Goodrich Trickel

The Osage in Missouri, by Kristie C. Wolferman

Paris, Tightwad, and Peculiar: Missouri Place Names, by Margot Ford McMillen

Quinine and Quarantine: Missouri Medicine through the Years, by Loren Humphrey

The Trail of Tears across Missouri, by Joan Gilbert

Immigrant Women
in the
Settlement
of Missouri

Robyn Burnett and
Ken Luebbering

University of Missouri Press
Columbia and London

Copyright © 2005 by
The Curators of the University of Missouri
University of Missouri Press, Columbia, Missouri 65201
Printed and bound in the United States of America

5 4 3 2 1   09 08 07 06 05

Library of Congress Cataloging-in-Publication Data

Burnett, Robyn.
Immigrant women in the settlement of Missouri / Robyn Burnett and Ken
Luebbering.
p. cm. — (Missouri heritage readers)
Summary: "Focuses on the lives of immigrant women in Missouri from the
colonial period to the Civil War to industrialization. Draws heavily on the
diaries, letters, and memoirs of immigrant women from many social classes and
ethnic backgrounds and contains photographs and narratives relating to
immigrant life"—Provided by publisher.
Includes bibliographical references and index.
ISBN 0-8262-1591-2 (alk. paper)
1. Women pioneers—Missouri—History. 2. Women immigrants—Missouri—
History. 3. Women pioneers—Missouri—Biography. 4. Women immigrants—
Missouri—Biography. 5. Pioneers—Missouri—History. 6. Immigrants—
Missouri—History. 7. Frontier and pioneer life—Missouri. 8. Missouri—Social
life and customs. 9. Missouri—Biography. 10. Missouri—Social life and
customs—Sources. I. Luebbering, Ken, 1946– II. Title. III. Series.
F466.B96 2005
977.8—dc22
2005005283

⊗™ This paper meets the requirements of the
American National Standard for Permanence of Paper
for Printed Library Materials, Z39.48, 1984.

Designer: Stephanie Foley
Typesetter: Foley Design
Printer and binder: Thomson-Shore, Inc.
Typeface: Goudy

To the tired, the poor, and the hungry—
those who came before and those who still come

Contents

Preface

We own an old quilt, a favorite for picnics, made of scraps of fabric. The pieces of flannel, corduroy, gingham, and denim are different sizes and shapes, different colors and textures, and are arranged in no particular pattern, but these assorted scraps somehow come together to create something pleasing and complete.

The metaphor of a historical patchwork quilt made of the lives of immigrant women stayed with us throughout our work on this book. Many women who came to Missouri lacked the ability, time, or inclination to leave written records, and the records they did leave are often fragmentary. However, there are many records of women's lives, from different kinds of sources, of different times, and about different kinds of women. Some of these records are tiny and seem inconsequential at first glance; some are voluminous. Some reflect common experiences; others tell extraordinary tales.

We set out to write a book that focused on immigrant women in nineteenth-century Missouri. However, the topic resisted being contained within tight chronological, geographic, or demographic borders. First, it seemed important to include information about Missouri's early French settlers. They were few in number; their entry into Missouri predated the nineteenth-century; and many were not themselves first-generation emigrants from Europe. Nevertheless, the French Catholic culture and customs brought by these early settlers provide an important and interesting context for the later immigration of women into the state. Similarly, we reject-ed the year 1900 as an arbitrary cutoff point for stories in the book,

because immigration in the first two decades of the twentieth century continued the patterns begun in the latter part of the nineteenth.

The geographic border proved porous, as well. For example, in
telling the story of immigrant women in Missouri, it seemed appropriate to discuss women in villages on the Illinois side of the Mississippi River, homesteads on the Kansas side of the Missouri River,
and immigrant neighborhoods in Kansas City, Kansas. Many immigrants who traveled through, conducted trade in, or worked in Missouri ultimately settled outside the state's borders. They, too, are
part of Missouri's history.

We also faced some demographic issues. Immigrant women's
lives are inextricably entwined with those of their fathers, husbands, sons, and brothers, and sometimes we have used the men's
stories to illustrate aspects of women's experiences. Finally, we considered the important question of whether to include African
American women in this work. In one sense, many were immigrants, but because of their forced migration, their enslavement,
and its aftermath, their experiences and life stories are significantly
different from those of the immigrants who chose to come to
America in search of better lives for themselves and their children.
We have occasionally made reference to African American women
when we had information that provided an interesting comparison
or context for immigrants of European descent, but we have not
considered them to be "immigrants" in the same sense. There were
some other non-European immigrants to Missouri in the nineteenth century, but they were almost exclusively male workers who
came without families.

If the stories we have stitched together in this historical quilt
seem to emphasize German immigrant women and the City of St.
Louis, this is no accident. The Germans made up by far the largest
immigrant group in Missouri. Unfortunately, among the Irish,
whose numbers made them a strong but distant second, stories of
individual women's lives proved harder to find. No doubt the relative size of these two groups partly accounts for this, but there were
also more middle-class, well-educated women among the Germans,

and such women were more likely to leave written records. Similarly, although immigrants settled throughout Missouri, St. Louis was unrivaled in its ability to draw immigrants.

It is important not to take an individual woman's story and generalize too broadly from it, but by taking what we know about many individual women, we have attempted to create a picture that has depth and meaning. These scraps seemed worth patching together because Missouri's immigrant women and their stories deserve to be remembered.

Acknowledgments

We are grateful to Becky Schroeder for her advice and assistance and to Dolf Schroeder for his generosity in allowing us access to his photographs. Thank you also to the staffs of Ellis Library at the University of Missouri–Columbia, the Missouri State Archives, the State Library, the Western Historical Manuscript Collection, the State Historical Society of Missouri in Columbia, the Missouri Historical Society, the Eden Theological Seminary Archives, and the Benedictine Convent of Perpetual Adoration for their help. Cindy Cotner at Ellis Library and Laura Jolley at the Missouri State Archives were particularly helpful and gracious with their time.

Immigrant Women in the Settlement of Missouri

Introduction

Elise Dubach was born in Switzerland in 1842. Her father, Benjamin, was the tenant of a dairy farm on the southern slope of *Montagne d'Orvin*. He owned two goats and five cows, which provided milk for their dairy; sheep, which provided the family with wool for winter garments; and a field of flax, which provided linen for summer clothing. He grew barley and cut hay to feed the dairy animals. The family earned income by selling butter in the nearby village of Orvin. Elise's mother, Jeanette, had a loom for weaving flax into linen shirts and dresses, wool into cloaks and stockings, and silkworm cocoons into "silk finery for Sunday."

In her memoir, *Sunbonnet Days*, published by her son Bliss Isley in 1935, Elise recalled her childhood as a happy time, and she described the rare beauty of the area in which they lived: "Below us wound the lovely valley of the Aare, beyond which towered the Alps, ever beautiful, whether veiled in clouds or ashimmer with the iridescent reflections of sunlight on the snow." She considered herself "rich in education," because her family had more books than any of their friends and she was able to speak and read both French and German. Their French-born mother spoke to Elise and her two younger brothers, Fred and Adolph, in French, and their father spoke to them in German. They were expected to reply as they were spoken to, so they were at ease in both languages. From the age of eight, Elise walked three miles down the mountain to Orvin to attend school, where classes were taught in French. By the time Elise was twelve, her mother had given her a practical education, too, teaching her to keep house and sew.

Elise Dubach in her wedding dress, taken
in St. Joseph in 1861. (Courtesy of John
Mattox)

The Dubach family was content. They considered themselves
well-off. Then a letter arrived one Saturday in the autumn of 1854
that would change their lives. It came from Elise's Uncle Christian,
who thought of his brother's family as poor.

Christian had immigrated to America in the late 1840s. He
worked as a cabinetmaker in Ste. Genevieve, where he married a
woman named Christine, and together they moved to St. Joseph.
Christian opened a wagon shop there, and Christine started a
boardinghouse. Both businesses prospered. Elise later wrote, "In a
single year they cleared more than three hundred dollars above all
expenses. This was almost too fabulous for credence, yet we believed
it, for did it not say so in Uncle's own handwriting?" When the
Kansas-Nebraska Act opened up new territories for homesteaders,
Christian thought this would be a great opportunity for his "poor
brother Benjamin."

Benjamin was preparing the roof of the house for winter when the letter arrived. While he undertook the annual chore of mending shingles and sweeping the summer's dirt from the roof, Jeanette delivered butter to the village. The mail she carried when she got home generated much excitement because getting a letter was a big event in those days. The children stood in the yard, and Benjamin came to the edge of the roof to listen while Jeanette read the letter aloud. The letter had long since been lost when *Sunbonnet Days* was written, but Elise remembered it well:

My dear brother:

You cannot do better than to come to America immediately. If you remain in Switzerland you will grow old without being any better off than you are today. Labor is so cheap and land is so dear with you, that no matter if you should live to be a hundred and have health and strength to work to your last day, you could even then have scarcely earned enough to buy yourself a farm to leave to your children.

With us, land is practically given away. With what money you can realize from the sale of your possessions, you can fit yourself out here as a farmer with implements, work animals, wagons and all of that.

Only last May President Pierce signed the Kansas-Nebraska Bill, converting part of the Indian lands into two new territories, Kansas and Nebraska. Kansas is just across the river from St. Joseph. All this summer people have been taking up lands within the very sight of this city. The laws allow a farmer to become owner of one hundred and sixty acres by living on it, by building a house on it, by cultivating the soil, and, at the end of five years, by paying only one dollar and a quarter an acre.

Because of nearness to St. Joseph the land is especially desirable, for St. Joseph affords a ready market. This city is the largest place between St. Louis and San Francisco and is destined to be the greatest city in western America. It is now the chief terminus for the California, Oregon, and Mormon trails. The Rocky Mountain trappers and the Indian traders of the plains are supplied from this market.

I suggest that you leave Orvin about February 1, which will

bring you here in April, in time to cross the Missouri River and select the farm you desire in the spring. The laws of the United States permit foreigners to take up land on the same terms as the citizens of this country. So generous are the Americans that they have even given the right to foreigners to vote in these two territories within six months after they have made their declaration of becoming citizens of the United States.

Benjamin Dubach grew more and more excited as the letter was read out. When it was finished, he threw his broom down from the roof and exclaimed: "Let the next tenant sweep this roof. Now, we are going to America."

And so they did. The Dubachs were not driven out of their home in Switzerland by poverty, famine, political strife, or religious persecution. They, like so many immigrants, were drawn to America by the promise of better lives in the New World.

Chapter 1

Immigrant Settlement in Missouri

⚜

When Meriwether Lewis and William Clark set off from St. Louis and started up the Missouri River in 1804 to explore the newly purchased Louisiana Territory, Europeans had already been living in what is now Missouri for much of the previous century. French settlers had founded several permanent communities near the Mississippi River. The first French to settle in Missouri came to mine lead. Later, farmers and merchants arrived, and around 1735 the community of Ste. Genevieve, Missouri's oldest permanent settlement, was established. After the Illinois territory came under British control in 1763, many French settlers moved from there to Missouri. By the time of the Louisiana Purchase, the main settlements in Missouri—Ste. Genevieve, Cape Girardeau, St. Charles, and St. Louis—were all French. Consequently, the laws and customs were French as well.

Some Americans had also settled in the area before the Louisiana Purchase, but afterward Americans began coming to the new territory in larger numbers. In 1804 the population of what would be Missouri was about 10,000; in 1810 it was almost twice that many, and by 1820 it had surpassed 66,000. Much of this increase resulted from the large migration west that began in earnest in 1814, following the War of 1812. Although some European immigrants arrived from Germany and Ireland, the vast majority of the

5

settlers were American. While the pre-1804 population was nearly half French, the new settlers "Americanized" the area. By the 1830 census, the first following statehood, Missouri was 90 percent American.

These Americans were largely descended from the earlier Scotch-Irish immigrants who had settled primarily in Pennsylvania, Virginia, and the Carolinas. Geographer Russel Gerlach reports that over a quarter million emigrants from northern Ireland came to colonial America between 1718 and 1775. It was from these areas that the great majority of the pioneers came to settle the new western territories. These American settlers gave the state its early southern culture and political bent.

According to Gerlach, there were two kinds of Ulstermen, as the descendants of the Scotch-Irish immigrants are sometimes called. The first he terms "low-culture," and these form our familiar image of the pioneer. They often lived by hunting and subsistence farming on land of marginal quality that was available free or for a nominal cost. As more settlers moved into their area, they frequently picked up stakes and moved on. They were the first to move west in large numbers, and they went with few belongings and less money. After several generations they arrived in Missouri, settling mostly in the Ozarks.

The second kind of Ulsterman, termed "high culture," was the southerner with more money, finer clothes, and, often, slaves. These families could afford the more fertile farmlands along the Mississippi and Missouri rivers, and some established commercial farms there. Others settled in St. Louis and set up businesses, changing it over time from a French village to a southern town. This second group was interested in education and religion and established schools and churches, mainly Presbyterian. The men of this group provided many of the business and political leaders in the early years of statehood.

The first large wave of foreign immigration began to arrive in Missouri in the 1830s. It was both heralded and precipitated by Gottfried Duden, who arrived in St. Louis in 1824. Duden spent nearly three years living on a farm in Warren County and record-

**Report on a Journey
to the Western States
of North America**

and a Stay of Several Years
Along the Missouri (During the
Years 1824, '25, '26, 1827)

Gottfried Duden

Cover of the English translation of Gottfried Duden's book, published by the University of Missouri Press in 1980. Duden's account of his stay in Missouri resulted in massive emigration from German-speaking countries. (A. E. Schroeder Collection)

ing his experiences there. After his return to Germany, he published *Report on a Journey to the Western States,* describing his experiences. His stay in Missouri coincided with a period of extremely mild weather, summer and winter. In addition, he was able to hire men to clear land, build fences, and do the rest of his farm labor while he wrote and visited his friendly American neighbors. Duden's book was one of about fifty relating to life in the United States pub-lished in the German states during the first half of the nineteenth century, and these books fired the imaginations of many Germans seeking better lives. "Emigration fever" took hold, infecting thou-sands of Germans.

Germans organized emigration societies to help potential emi-grants arrange their journeys to America. Several large groups of Germans came to Missouri as a result of the work of these societies. In addition, some settlement groups were made up almost entirely of German-speakers from the eastern United States. The "White Water Dutch," for example, arrived in Cape Girardeau from North Carolina as early as 1800. When the German Settlement Society of Philadelphia founded Hermann in the late 1830s, they envisioned a grand city in the West where German language and customs would be maintained.

Not all new German immigrants to Missouri settled in St. Louis, but virtually all of them passed through it because the city served as a transportation hub for the land to the west. Some stayed only long enough to earn money to buy land or to make arrangements to travel farther into the state. Some stayed permanently. By the 1840s so many Germans lived in St. Louis that one new immigrant, Emil Mallinckrodt, wrote his brother in Germany that he heard so much German spoken on the streets and saw so many Germans about in the city that he could imagine himself back in Germany. Further-more, the Germans he saw were successful. "They own one-third of St. Louis," he wrote. "We live here as if in Germany, wholly sur-rounded by Germans." The ranks of the new German immigrants provided St. Louis with countless skilled craftsmen, stonemasons, carpenters, and brewers, for example, and many founded businesses. By 1850 Germans actually outnumbered Americans in St. Louis.

Others traveled farther west with most settling on the land along the Missouri River between St. Louis and Jefferson City. So many Germans settled there that the area became known as the Missouri Rhineland. They established farms and vineyards around villages near the river. Many Germans had enough money to buy good land or could earn it fairly quickly once they arrived in America.

Between 1830 and 1860 they transformed the fertile river valleys of the state into a veritable rural German landscape, dotted with substantial stone and wooden houses and barns on farms and clustered in villages. It seemed there was a Catholic, Lutheran, or Evangelical church perched on the most prominent hill in each town, providing both a physical and symbolic center to the community.

Their farms and the towns and villages they supported prospered, and by 1860 the frontier that had drawn them, as well as the earlier Scotch-Irish, to Missouri had passed to the west. Besides St. Louis and the Missouri River valley, the areas of heaviest German concentration were along the Mississippi River, north of St. Louis in St. Charles, Lincoln, and Pike counties and in the southeast in Perry, Cape Girardeau, and Ste. Genevieve counties. Smaller concentrations of Germans settled in other areas, such as Bethel in northeast Missouri. Although there had been a handful of other immigrants such as Poles, Bohemians, and Belgians before the Civil War, the communities they established were quickly overrun by the waves of Germans. Still others, such as the Cornish and Welsh miners who came in the early years of statehood, remained in the state only a few years before moving on to find work in other states.

Near the end of the 1840s Missouri began to see another kind of immigrant. Poor Irish who were fleeing the disaster of the Irish potato famine typically arrived in St. Louis with no money. Most came from rural areas, and they had few skills useful in an urban environment. With no money, and no way to earn much, they could not buy farms, and they faced a situation only slightly less harsh than that they had fled. These Irish were different from the earlier Scotch-Irish in several important ways. First, they were Roman Catholics arriving in a predominantly Protestant city and were the object of religious fears and prejudices. Second, they were seen both by themselves and others as being "foreigners," not Americans. Third, their experiences on Irish tenant farms had not taught them how to live on marginal land. Although there were a few attempts to establish rural Irish communities, led in part by a Father John Hogan, none of the communities survived, and virtually all of Missouri's Irish immigrants settled in cities and towns.

The Civil War temporarily disrupted large-scale immigration, but it quickly resumed after the war's end. In 1865 the Missouri General Assembly created the state Board of Immigration to publish information describing the state's resources and advantages and to appoint agents to travel through eastern states and Europe, promoting and aiding immigration to Missouri. When large numbers of new immigrants began arriving in the 1870s, more came from southern and eastern Europe than before, but the Germans and Irish remained the overwhelming majority until the end of the century. The later immigrants swelled the population of St. Louis and also filled in less-populated rural parts of the state. About 45 percent of St. Louis's population was foreign-born in 1870. In the state as a whole, the number of foreign-born residents grew from about 160,000 in 1860 to more than 234,000 in 1890. Almost half lived in St. Louis, and more than half of those were German. By contrast Jackson County, with the second largest number of foreign-born, had only 22,000. At the end of the century, Germans still made up the majority of Missouri's immigrant population; the Irish, with about 15 percent, were the second largest group.

Immigration to rural Missouri after the Civil War was fostered by the recruitment of immigrants by the railroads, which were extending their tracks dramatically. From 1865 to 1890, the number of miles of track in the state grew from eight hundred to more than six thousand. Railroads needed settlements along the new lines to provide workers, goods to transport, and markets for goods produced elsewhere. As a result they recruited both in Europe and the eastern states to bring people into these areas. Their efforts brought more diversity to rural Missouri, depositing pockets of Bohemians, Scandinavians, Slavs, Hungarians, and Italians around the state. For example, Danes and Swedes settled near Rolla. Slightly to the east, Welsh and Irish settlers worked the clay and iron deposits. More Germans came during this period as well, most notably to St. Joseph and the southwestern part of the state, including Joplin and Freistatt. Some of the Freistatt settlers were new immigrants, and some were second- or third-generation Americans of German descent from Minnesota, Wisconsin, and Illinois. They chose this

The Great Southwest!

Central and Southwest Missouri,

Possessing all the requirements of good climate, good soil and good health—with varied and beautiful scenery, and springs, and streams of pure water running rapidly over rocky bottoms—with long, yet cool summers, and short and mild winters, invites

Emigration from all other States, and from Europe,

Come from the cold regions of all countries, where winter consumes all the products of summer; come from localities afflicted with consumption, to a place where pulmonary disease is almost unknown, except in the cases cured by its climate; come from crowded cities where the laboring man is poor, to a region where industry is sure of reward, where a home is easily obtained, and wealth always within the reach of humble men; come from high priced lands of the North to the cheap, yet better lands of Central and Southwest Missouri.

—THE—

Atlantic & Pacific Railroad Co.,

—OWN—

1,150,000 Acres of Land,

Which they offer cheap, on long credit, and with free transportation over their Road to all purchasers. The greatest inducements offered to men who will organize Colonies! Village Plats, where are expensive depots and side tracts, and centers already of considerable trade, offered for sale by the acre on long credit. Colonists can obtain reduced rates from all points to St. Louis, whence this Company will provide tickets and transportation.

For particulars, in pamphlets and maps, apply to

A. L. DEANE, Land Commissioner,

25 South Fourth Street, St. Louis.

Railroad companies used advertisements such as this one in newspapers and on handbills as a way of attracting settlers to land near railway lines. (State Historical Society of Missouri, Columbia)

site for a new settlement because the Frisco railroad was selling land to homesteaders for six dollars an acre. In the same area, a group of Polish immigrants transformed Bricefield into Pulaskifield. One of the last groups to arrive as part of the railroad expansion formed an Italian community at Knobview in the 1890s (later renamed Rosati), resulting in the development of one of the most important areas of the state's wine industry.

More eastern Europeans came to Missouri in the later decades of the century, mostly to St. Louis, but the numbers remained small. After 1900, however, eastern Europeans began to arrive in numbers large enough to create viable communities. Although there were some immigrant communities founded around the turn of the century in Kansas City and St. Joseph, neither of those cities ever became immigrant cities in the way that St. Louis did. For the most part, these later immigrants remained in St. Louis, which saw the development of a number of vibrant immigrant communities. The Hill became home to a large concentration of Italians; Bohemian Hill was settled by Czechs, Austrians, Hungarians, Slovaks, Croats, and Serbs. Many neighborhoods centered on churches: Bohemian Hill around St. John Nepomuk, for example, or the Greek neighborhood around St. Nicholas Greek Orthodox Church.

Although immigrants continued to come to the state and to enrich its economy and culture, by 1920 the great waves of immigration had ended, and the patchwork of Missouri's ethnic quilt had been essentially stitched into place.

Chapter 2

Women Immigrants

꙾

I mmigrant women's experiences in America were different from men's in significant ways. Maxine Schwartz Seller, editor of *Immigrant Women*, says that like immigrant men, "women faced poverty, loneliness, discrimination, and physical danger as they struggled to build new lives in a new land. But their identity as women shaped the roles, opportunities, and experiences available to them in the family, the workplace, the community, and the nation."

This was certainly true for the women who came to Missouri in the nineteenth century, as the stories in this book will illustrate. Not all Missouri's immigrant women were alike, of course, and their experiences were as diverse as the women themselves. Nevertheless, some general comments about immigrant women may be helpful.

Most immigrant women, like most immigrant men, were motivated to come to America to improve their economic situation. Others came in search of political or religious freedom. Whether their primary motivation was economic, political, or religious, they often came because they believed their children would have better lives in America. Anna and Anton Pointek found life unbearable in occupied Poland in the years after the failed revolution of 1863. They came to America because they wanted to raise their children in a free society. According to a history of Pulaskifield, the Pointeks saved money for three years, but they still did not have enough to pay for the passage of all five of their children. Anna could not bear to leave any of her children behind, so they devised a scheme that would allow them to make the journey together. Anton Jr. worked as a dishwasher on the ship to pay for his passage, and Anna and Anton punched holes in the lid of a trunk and smuggled one of their younger children onboard the ship inside it. Once in Missouri, the Pointeks farmed land just outside Pulaskifield. They changed their name to Friday, the English translation of their Polish name, but they spoke Polish at home and maintained their Polish customs.

Like Anna Pointek, most immigrant women came to Missouri as part of a family unit. Many came to America to begin their married life. Some married before leaving Europe, others after their arrival in the New World. One of Missouri's early Jewish settlers, Rachel Block, was engaged to Nathan Abeles while still in Europe. However, they did not marry because Nathan was too poor to support a family. They traveled together to Louisiana, Missouri, where Nathan left Rachel with her brothers, Phineas and Jacob. When he was unable to find a job as a clerk in St. Louis, Nathan became a peddler. He started with only fourteen dollars, and within a year he had enough money to marry his fiancée. He had been unable to afford the marriage fees in Bohemia, but in Missouri the license cost only twenty-five cents.

When Italian immigrant Rosa Cassettari traveled to Missouri in the 1880s to join her husband in a mining camp, one of her traveling companions, Francesa, was coming to marry a man she had never met. The young women were from Lombardy, but Francesa did not mind that she would be marrying a Tuscan. "She was so happy she was going to America and going to get married that she didn't care who the man was," Rosa said.

Sometimes a woman brought a dowry or property to a marriage that helped pay for the journey to America or establish the couple in the New World. An unmarried woman with financial prospects could be an attractive partner. Swedish immigrant Joseph Andersson arrived in Dallas County without a wife and found no eligible prospects among the two or three Swedish families in the immedi-

Mary Roziak Sunderlik with her son, John, and daughter, Mary, just before leaving Slovakia in 1909 to join her husband, Julius, in Ilasco. (Courtesy of Armenia Engelmeyer)

ate area. He enlisted a friend in nearby Hickory County to help him find a wife. In 1886 the friend wrote to him: "I wish that you would come over here for a visit. I have another girl for you. This one has her full reason, is able to manage a household, and make a man happy indeed. I have talked to her and to her father about you and if you can win the girl's heart, you would attain both a fine wife and a farm in the bargain."

Terence Pihlblad, who edited and published some of the Swedish immigrants' letters from Dallas County, reports that Joseph's attempt to find a Swedish bride failed. He married an American woman from Polk County instead.

Wives often remained in Europe while their husbands came to Missouri to work. Wilhelm Niggemeir worked as a shoemaker in St. Louis until he had saved enough money to send for his wife and five children. In 1848 he wrote a letter advising his wife how to prepare for the journey, detailing the food and cooking equipment she would need on the ship and warning her repeatedly to keep a close watch on the children so that they would not fall overboard. Similarly, William Norton, a Bohemian who settled near Hawk Point in the 1850s, worked in St. Louis until he had enough money to send for his family. William (whose name was originally Vaclaw Novotny) established a home for them in Lincoln County and continued to work in St. Louis while they managed the farm. He went home twice a year to take his pay.

Some married women came reluctantly to the New World. Luise Marbach, one of the Saxon Lutheran settlers who came to Missouri in 1839, opposed the plan to immigrate to America from the outset. During the Atlantic crossing, Pastor Martin Stephan, the group's leader, ordered that she be separated from her husband, Franz, and detained in her cabin because he was concerned about her negative influence on Franz. This was particularly brutal because two of the Marbach children had died while Franz was away from home making arrangements for the trip, and their two-year-old son, Martin, died during the early part of the Atlantic journey. Furthermore, Luise was pregnant at the time of the journey. The couple's forced separation continued after they reached New Orleans and during the journey up the Mississippi River to Missouri. Two more Marbach children died after they settled in Perry County. Luise, Franz, and their two remaining children returned to Germany in 1841.

Although such accounts are unusual, some women actually refused to come to America with their husbands. One of the early Jewish settlers in St. Louis, Wolf Block, originally immigrated to Baltimore in the 1790s. He was successful as a merchant there and returned to Bohemia to get his wife. However, she refused to leave her home and divorced him instead. He returned to Baltimore without her and migrated to St. Louis around 1816, according to Walter Ehrlich, who chronicled the history of early Jewish settlers in St. Louis in *Zion in the Valley.*

Sometimes a married woman emigrated without her husband, but such cases must have been rare. Forty-year-old Johanna Christiane Nagel left her husband and younger children to join the Saxon Lutherans in the late 1830s. Her oldest son went with her. She later regretted her decision, however, and in 1842 she petitioned the congregation of Trinity Lutheran Church in St. Louis for financial assistance to return to her abandoned family. They granted her request, and she and her son went home.

Widows sometimes immigrated to Missouri with their children. Anna Maria Ilsabein Bonsen married Friedrich Wilhelm Landwehr in the Jollenbeck region of Prussia in 1837. Friedrich died in 1859, leaving Anna with five children to raise. Later that year, the Landwehrs traveled to Franklin County, where Anna's sister and other German immigrants lived. They arrived at the end of November, with winter approaching. According to family records, the sister's house was too small for both families, and a month after her arrival, Anna married a forty-two-year-old widower with five children of his own to raise. Her older boys found jobs in the area that provided room and board. Her fifteen-year-old daughter went to work in St. Louis. The family records do not indicate whether Anna and her husband knew each other before her arrival in Franklin County. Perhaps the sister with the small house helped arrange this marriage, either before or after Anna's arrival in Missouri.

Two other widows who immigrated to Missouri were Annie Posler and her daughter, Josephine Praszak. Annie's son, John, first emigrated from Bohemia to the United States in 1850. After living in Wisconsin and Iowa for a number of years, he moved to Cainsville (then Cains Mill) in Harrison County in north central Missouri. He was the first Bohemian to settle in the area. After serving in the Civil War, he returned to Bohemia to get his mother and his sister. John had his own farm, but he bought another 120 acres for Josephine and her two daughters. Grant Leazenby, who recorded his memories of the Czech immigrants in Harrison County, recalled that after Josephine died, John took care of his two orphaned nieces as well as his mother. In 1872, John married Anna Skakal, a member of one of the several Bohemian families who had moved into the Cainsville area after his arrival.

Single women immigrated to America, too. Sometimes they traveled alone and paid their own fares for the Atlantic crossing. In the 1840s, in the German province of Westphalia, the four young daughters of the Ahlers family were placed in foster homes after their mother died. They had to work for their keep. Frederika was the first to decide to emigrate. While still in her teens she wove sails to earn enough money for her passage to America. In 1852 she left home alone. She found lodging in St. Louis with a German she met when her boat docked, and she worked in the city for a year before moving to Gasconade County. In 1853 Frederika married a man she had known in Westphalia, John Caspar Cordes, a widower with a young son. They farmed and ran a store at Bay for a number of years, and they had eight more children. Frederika's three sisters immigrated to Missouri in the late 1850s; two of them joined her, and one stayed in St. Louis.

Unmarried women sometimes emigrated to avoid an unwanted marriage, as was the case with Sophie Luise Weitbrecht. Sophie did not escape marriage altogether by emigrating, however, because on her voyage across the Atlantic she met an Evangelical Lutheran minister who was on his way to a German church in Red Bud, Illinois, and she married him two days after their arrival in New Orleans.

Once they arrived in Missouri, whether they settled in the wilderness, small towns, or city neighborhoods, immigrant women faced common problems. Their new environment was unfamiliar and often dangerous. Food, clothing, and customs were strange. Besides adjusting to all those things, most immigrant women had to learn English. Sometimes a woman found that the values of American society were in conflict with her own. Seller says, "Whatever their point of departure and whatever their destination, for most women the changes in their lives were so radical that their initial years in America were consumed by a struggle for physical and psychological survival." Although conditions varied depending on the women's circumstances, there were inevitably hardships to be endured. Survival itself was nearly always a challenge.

Childbirth was a great peril for women in the nineteenth century. This was true, of course, for women in Europe as well, but immigrant women faced some added risks. Women on the frontier sometimes gave birth unassisted by a doctor, a midwife, or even another woman. Immigrant women generally had a greater chance of dying in childbirth than did American-born women, according to Doris Weatherford, author of *Foreign and Female: Immigrant Women in America, 1840–1930*. There are several reasons for this, including more frequent pregnancies, inadequate care during and immediately after pregnancy, and unsanitary conditions during childbirth, which increased the risk of infection.

Although Missouri's frontier years were long past, Italian immigrant Rosa Cassettari gave birth alone in a mining camp near Union in the 1880s. Rosa and her baby survived, but many other women were not so fortunate. Johanne Christiane Henrietta Buerger from Lunzenau in Saxony settled in Seelitz in Perry County. In the summer of 1840, the new community was hard hit by illness. At one time the entire Buerger family—Johanne, her husband, Pastor E. M. Buerger, and their two young boys—were ill with fever and did not even have an adequate supply of drinking water. In October Johanne gave birth without the assistance of a doctor or a midwife. The child died at birth and Johanne died two weeks later. Polish immigrant Kathrine Abramovitz and her husband, John, who settled on land near Pierce City in 1873, raised six children and then raised their granddaughter Rose because their daughter Eve died shortly after giving birth to her.

Husbands who were left behind when their wives died needed help immediately, especially when there were young children to care for and no older children able to step in and assume the mother's work or extended family to call on for assistance. Whether they

"Say not goodnight, but in a brighter world bid me good morning." Child's tombstone near Cainsville. (A. E. Schroeder Collection)

lived in urban or rural areas in Europe or America, women did much of the domestic work essential to keep families fed and clothed. Linda Pickle notes that "when women died as a result of childbirth, illness or years of exertion, other immigrant women often took their place caring for the family."

Homesickness was often a great problem for women immigrants who had left their families and friends in Europe. Most knew they would never return to their original homes and would never see their family members again. Loneliness compounded homesickness for women in isolated frontier settlements. While living in the Westphalia settlement, Jette Bruns lamented the absence of a female friend in a letter to her brother Heinrich: "How lonely I am here, no female being who thinks as I do, with whom I can now and then exchange my feelings when I need that kind of refreshment, when I would like to forget the daily troubles and sorrows, when these could be set aside for a short time." Henry Bode remembered his mother, Elizabeth Kirsch Bode, sitting by the window of their home weeping with homesickness on many occasions.

Seller says that for many women "children were the welcome antidote to the loneliness of immigration." However, many children did not survive, and the death of children was particularly difficult for women. In September 1841 dysentery struck Jette Bruns's family in Westphalia. The whole family was afflicted with the illness. On September 13 her two-year-old daughter, Johanna, died. Six days later her four-year-old son, Max, died. On October 2 the baby, Rudolph, died, twelve days after they thought he had recovered. In November she wrote: "How I wish I could have said farewell to the world six weeks ago. . . . It really hit me too hard that I also had to lose little Rudolph." According to Adolf Schroeder, who edited a collection of Jette's letters with Carla Schulz-Geisberg, "the deaths of her children, for whose future she had left her home, devastated her." Years later, when Jette wrote her autobiography, she reported that it had taken them a long time to recover from these events. She said, "Finally my dear husband exhorted me with all his strength that I still had some duties to tend to."

Pauline Muehl, one of Hermann's early settlers, bore eight children in just over ten years. In 1849 her four-year-old daughter, Thusnelda, died from cholera. In 1854 cholera struck the family again. Pauline's husband, Eduard, died on July 7 at 1:30 in the afternoon. Her daughter Rosa, not quite four, died about four hours later. On August 31, her oldest son, Hermann, also died. She recorded these events in her husband's notebook, but she did not record her feelings about them. In February 1855 Pauline gave birth to another boy. She recorded the birth in the notebook and wrote: "I have in all 5 children, and if it is only God's will, I can hopefully live to see in them great joy."

Immigrant women endured many hardships. They survived malnutrition, disease, and childbirth. Some lived in poverty until the end of their lives and struggled through periods of homesickness, loneliness, and grief. Others gradually became more financially secure, more comfortable, even happy in the New World. Many always believed that life in America was better than what they had left behind. Seller says that "many mothers took comfort in the thought that their children would never know the hunger and oppression they had experienced in the old world—and the loneliness they suffered in the new."

Chapter 3

Women in Early French Villages

ஃ

C hristian Schultz, a German traveler who visited villages west of the Mississippi during his trip to America in 1807 and 1808, did not form a favorable impression of the French settlers he met there. He wrote that the area around Old Mines was "a very unpleasant place" and that the inhabitants quarreled and brawled so much that it amounted to "a constant scene of warfare."

The inhabitants of Ste. Genevieve, in contrast, celebrated far too much, he thought. "One ball follows another so close in succession," he wrote, "that I have often wondered how the ladies were enabled to support themselves under this violent exercise, which is here carried to extremes. The balls are generally opened at candlelight, and continue till ten or twelve the next day." He also commented that Sundays in the village were more days of amusement than of religious solemnity. While he admitted that there was a high mass every Sunday, he was shocked that it lasted only half an hour, after which the inhabitants went about their business, whether that be work or amusement. Henry Brackenridge, who had lived in Ste. Genevieve as a child in the 1790s, later praised the residents for their "tame and peaceful disposition" but also called them "indolent and uninformed."

Most of the people whose behavior so amazed these visitors were not emigrants from France. Rather, they were predominantly third-

Ste. Genevieve in 1735. (Mural by O. E. Berninghaus, State Historical Society of Missouri, Columbia)

and fourth-generation French Canadians who had moved south, first into Illinois and later across the Mississippi, where they founded Missouri's earliest European settlements. Ste. Genevieve, the state's first permanent settlement, was an offshoot of the French villages across the river in Illinois and was probably established by 1735, although there are conflicting historical records on the year.

The comments by Schultz and Brackenridge indicate that these French villages were substantially different from other settlements these writers knew. Life proceeded at a different pace in the French villages than in American ones. Celebrations such as those mentioned by Schultz were not constant, but seasonal. Schultz stayed there only briefly, when he was stranded during a harsh winter by a frozen Mississippi River. His hosts built him a boat so he could leave at the first opportunity when the spring thaw finally came; they were no doubt as glad of his departure as he was.

His visit coincided with one of the major festival times for the French, the period from Christmas to Lent. Because Lent lasts almost two months and was then a solemn season of religious penitence during which celebrations were forbidden, people used the cold winter weeks to enjoy themselves while they could. The festive season began with midnight mass on Christmas Eve. For the

Protestant boy, Henry Brackenridge, an earlier observer, it was awe-inspiring:

> At Christmas Eve, it was the custom to keep the church open all night, and at midnight to say mass. On this occasion, I found myself alone for nearly an hour before that time, seated on a high chair, or stool, with a cross in my hand, in front of the altar, which was splendidly decorated, and lighted with the largest wax candles the village could afford. My imagination was at first filled with an indescribable awe, at the situation in which I was placed, and I gazed upon the sacred images about the altar as if they were in reality what they represented.

After midnight mass came *Le Reveillon*, the traditional "wake-up" breakfast, which often lasted well into Christmas Day.

On New Year's Eve young people in costume went from house to house collecting pledges of food for the celebration of Epiphany, or Twelfth Night, on January 6, the traditional end of the twelve days of Christmas. While the young people went through the village, they sang "La Guignolée" a traditional begging song "not asking for very much," perhaps a bone of meat "only ninety feet long" or instead of food perhaps "only the oldest daughter of the house" whose feet they promised to keep warm. The singing was, of course, accompanied by much laughter and drinking.

Except during Lent, Sundays were a day of public activity in the villages. After attending mass in the morning, people gathered for public auctions or to conduct business, discuss community matters, and gossip. Many Sunday afternoons included dancing and games. These Sunday social activities contrasted markedly with behavior in Anglo-American communities, where religious citizens believed in refraining from both social activities and business matters on the Sabbath.

In Ste. Genevieve dances were held in the homes of the wealthier families, where there was enough space. Although residential lots in the French villages were usually large, houses were quite small by modern standards, even those of the wealthy. A house belonging to

Jean Baptiste Vallé house, originally built ca. 1793 and modified in the nineteenth century. Jean Baptiste was the commanding officer in Ste. Genevieve when the United States took control of the Louisiana Territory. He was one of the brothers-in-law of Pélagie Carpentier Vallé who fought her for custody of her children. (Missouri State Archives)

an important Ste. Genevieve family around 1800 might measure only six hundred square feet and be occupied by an average family of five. Carl Ekberg, author of *Colonial Ste. Genevieve: An Adventure on the Mississippi Frontier,* describes a typical lot, including "a cow barn, a stable, a henhouse, a corncrib, an orchard, a vegetable garden, a bake oven, a well, sometimes a slave's quarters, and occasionally a detached free-standing kitchen." Noticeably absent from this list is a privy, suggesting that the French preferred to use chamber pots instead. Only a few of the wealthiest families had separate kitchens; usually cooking was done in an open fireplace in the main room in the house.

The list also suggests that the French villagers had more variety in their diets than most Anglo-Americans did. American families on the frontier usually subsisted on a diet of fried meat, often game, cornbread, and milk. Henry Brackenridge described how meals prepared by the French women differed from those he was used to. "With the poorest French peasant, cookery is an art well understood. They make great use of vegetables, and prepared in a manner to be wholesome and palatable. Instead of roast and fried, they had soups and fricassees and gumbos and a variety of other dishes." To accompany these dishes they had maple sugar, honey, wine, beer, cider, and wheat bread (thinking cornbread fit only for "savages") and salads during the summer. Desserts were made from fruit and dairy products and included tarts, custards, and cheeses. One native food that quickly became a favorite among the French was watermelon. Gardens produced cabbage, peas, fresh beans, carrots, parsnips, cucumbers, radishes, onions, and squash. Other foods were added in the nineteenth century, including potatoes and tomatoes, which had previously been considered poisonous. Management of the gardens and orchards that provided this variety of food for the table was the province of the women.

Farmland was located outside the village in a common field. The French did not follow the American pattern of an isolated house on each farmstead. Pasture and woodlands were held in common and shared by all the villagers. Fields produced crops requiring more space than the village gardens could accommodate. Here the farmers grew wheat, oats, barley, and corn, as well as beans, turnips, pumpkins, and melons. Families also grew enough tobacco and cotton for their own needs.

In addition to gardening and cooking, French women performed some chores with the animals, gathering eggs and milking cows, for example. One task normally carried out by Anglo-American women at the time that the French did not engage in was weaving. Perhaps due to old prohibitions against home weaving, French households normally bought the fabric needed to make the family's clothes. Clothing followed old French traditions—for example, both men and women covered their heads with blue handkerchiefs—but incorporated some Native American items, such as deerskin breeches for the men and leather moccasins for both sexes.

Life in the villages was anything but idyllic. Many children died.

In Ste. Genevieve, the village with the most extensive and reliable records, infant mortality was very high. In the eighteenth century, an estimated one-third of babies died before reaching their first birthday; fewer than half reached adulthood. Often a village experienced a high number of deaths in a very short period. For three years in the late eighteenth century, the number of deaths in Ste. Genevieve was more than twice the normal rate. In each year, the peak came in the fall months, probably as the result of a combination of diseases such as dysentery and yellow fever. While these epidemics took those of all ages, children were particularly susceptible.

In the absence of physicians, women were the primary medical caregivers in the villages. In the late 1700s Marie Carpentier Vallé, a member of one of the settlement's most prominent families, took care of many sick children. She reportedly never refused to help when called by the mother of a sick child, no matter the time of day or night or the status of the family, and she never expected payment. For many ailments there were folk remedies of various kinds, but often all that could be done was to provide comfort until the disease had run its course.

The status of women in these settlements was complicated. As in American areas, husbands were the assumed heads of the households. On the other hand, most property in French marriages was legally held to be joint property, and women's signatures commonly appear on contracts for the sale of real estate and slaves. The Vallé family left sufficient records to provide an interesting insight into the place of women in French colonial society. Marianne Vallé regularly transacted business both with her husband François and independently, once bidding at an estate auction against the men in the crowd. It is not entirely clear if a married woman could conduct family business without her husband's permission. Documents exist that explicitly give a woman that permission, but that does not mean it would have been impossible without it. Almost certainly, a husband did not need his wife's permission, as in the case of François providing a dowry for his illegitimate daughter.

This case illustrates another aspect of women's status. The girl, who was raised in the Vallé household and publicly acknowledged, represents but one instance of children born to male white citizens and female African slaves. We know of no instances in these communities of white women giving birth to children of black fathers, although that in itself is not proof that such liaisons did not exist. It does indicate a sexual double standard, however, and it is hard to imagine an illegitimate daughter of Marianne's, white or black, being raised by François.

An unhappily married woman faced a difficult legal situation. Although separation was possible, divorce for any reason was illegal. Consequently, a woman could not entirely free herself of a problem husband. When Charles Vallé was squandering the family's money on gambling, drinking, and other women, his wife, Pélagie Carpentier Vallé, took him to court to prevent the complete loss of the family fortune. She was granted a separation, but when she wanted to leave for Canada with her children, the same judge who had granted the separation gave Pélagie's two brothers-in-law the right to take her children by force and keep them in Missouri.

As with the women who immigrated to Missouri in later decades, the early French settlers' lives were a mixture of joy and sadness, success and failure. In the years immediately following the Louisiana Purchase, they saw their culture overwhelmed by the new English-speaking Americans who flooded into the territory.

Chapter 4

Women in Colonial St. Louis

ॐ

I n 1763 the governor of Louisiana granted Maxent, Laclède and Company a monopoly to trade with Indians in Missouri. Colonel Antoine Maxent was one of the richest merchants in New Orleans; Pierre Laclède was the company's field agent. Laclède traveled up the Mississippi River on a keelboat with Auguste Chouteau, the fourteen-year-old son of his partner, Marie Thérèse Bourgeois Chouteau, and thirty employees to establish a trading post. They founded the colonial outpost that was to become St. Louis on a sloping, elevated site on the west bank of the Mississippi just south of its confluence with the Missouri River. The land had natural drainage; timber was plentiful; and there were grassy tracts nearby suitable for farming.

The founding group that arrived in the winter of 1764 included no women. Madame Chouteau joined Laclède later in the year after giving birth to their fourth child in New Orleans. When Laclède arrived, most of the French settlers in the area, mainly farmers and fur traders, were living in small communities on the eastern side of the Mississippi. He invited the French families in Illinois to join him in building his new settlement, offering free building lots in the village and land for farming on the outskirts. One of the first women to move into St. Louis was Margaret Blondeau Guion, who relocated from Cahokia with her husband, a

Marie Thérèse Bourgeois Chouteau. (Missouri Historical Society, St. Louis)

stonemason. Over the next two years, some fifty families moved into the village.

Like the French settlers in Ste. Genevieve, Creole families in St. Louis established a compact community surrounded by common crop- and pastureland. The street plan Laclède's men laid out was similar to that of other French and Spanish river towns, with large house plots along three streets parallel to the Mississippi. A few homes, including Laclède's, were made of stone, but most were built with upright logs, chinked with mortar, and covered with white-washed plaster. Each house had four small rooms in the corners that all opened into a large central room. They had porches and fenced-in backyards with gardens, fruit trees, and outbuildings. When Father Sebastian Meurin, a Jesuit frontier missionary, visited Laclède's settlement in 1766, he baptized four children in a tent because there was no church. The first church was built in 1770.

St. Louis was then the capital of Upper Louisiana and the garrison town for the Spanish government. It was a rendezvous point for hunters, boatmen, and fur company agents. Fur trading provided St. Louis's economic base for nearly three-quarters of a century. Nearly all expeditions outfitted there, and most of the fur destined for markets in the eastern United States or Europe passed through St. Louis. Thus, St. Louis was the focal point for activities that spanned north to the Canadian border and west nearly to the Pacific Ocean.

St. Louis grew slowly in its first decades. At the beginning of the nineteenth century, the village had only 925 inhabitants, including 268 slaves. Although the region as a whole grew somewhat more during this period, the village itself remained small and predominately French. When the United States took possession of St. Louis in 1804, two-thirds of the people in the town were cousins.

Historian Katharine Corbett describes the lives of women in colonial St. Louis in her book *In Her Place: A Guide to St. Louis Women's History*. She argues that childbearing and women's domestic skills were essential to the community's survival. There were far fewer women than men in early St. Louis, although the ratio of men to women had fallen to two to one by 1794. Women usually married before the age of twenty, often to men many years older. They bore many children, one-third of whom died in infancy.

The women of the village were mostly wives and daughters of merchants, traders, and craftsmen. St. Louis merchants accumulated property, including slaves, and created a network of kinship to protect their wealth. Corbett says: "It was the responsibility of young elite women to marry these homegrown aristocrats or their sons, produce children, and nurture family alliances." Pierre Laclède never married Marie Thérèse Chouteau, but their three daughters, Marie Pelagie, Marie Louise, and Victoire, married men of St. Louis's merchant class. The three daughters had a total of thirty-two children, twenty-four of whom lived to adulthood. Laclède and Chouteau's grandchildren, including those produced by the wives of Auguste and Pierre Chouteau, created a wealthy and powerful family network.

Madame Chouteau, with some initial help from Laclède and their sons, became one of the wealthiest people in the village. She owned a large farm that produced wheat, tobacco, corn, and livestock, and she traded in land, furs, and grain. Slaves did much of the work of the large Chouteau household and farm. Corbett notes that while hardships were common to all women at the end of the eighteenth century, wealthy women did not suffer from material deprivation or constant drudgery. A steady supply of goods, both necessities and luxuries, arrived in St. Louis on the boats that carried furs away to ship to international markets. Marie Thérèse Chouteau wore imported clothes and jewelry and ate from French china. In 1775, according to William Foley, author of *The First Chouteaus: River Barons of Early St. Louis,* her husband, René Chouteau, took legal action in an attempt to force her to return to New Orleans. A St. Louis official advised her to distance herself from Laclède and move outside the village to her farm. She did, although Laclède kept a room in her house there. She lived to be more than eighty years old, never giving up her independence. She freed her personal slave, Thérèse, in her will and left her some flour, a cow, a calf, and a small amount of money. At the time of her death in 1814, more than fifty grandchildren lived within a mile of her home.

Life in St. Louis during this era was largely regulated by a mixture of French and Spanish customs, class values, and legal traditions. Free women in colonial St. Louis had more property rights than women governed by American laws. Unlike laws based on the English tradition, which favored firstborn sons, in St. Louis sons and daughters were equally entitled to property. Thus, wives often brought property of their own to a marriage. Marriage contracts that

Whether in St. Louis, Ste. Genevieve, or the French villages in Illinois, dancing was an important social activity. Henry Brackenridge called the balls "schools of manners for the children." (State Historical Society of Missouri, Columbia)

protected women's property were common. However, laws that protected a woman's assets did not protect her from the authority of her husband in other matters. For example, a husband had the legal right to physically abuse his wife and to make decisions affecting her and their children.

There is scant record of women's daily lives in colonial St. Louis. Most women—and most men—were illiterate and did not leave personal records such as letters or diaries. Corbett says that wealthy women who owned black or Indian slaves "probably did plenty of home management and little direct domestic labor." Large family gatherings were common, and guests often stayed for months. Furthermore, most business transactions took place in the home. Merchants and traders who spent lengthy periods of time away from home often left their wives in charge of business while they were away.

Less affluent women did their own housework and earned money or traded for goods and services by taking in laundry or providing room and board for the boatmen and trappers who passed through the village. Women also served as midwives and nursed the sick. Some free black women bought land on which they grew produce to sell.

There were also slave women—blacks, Indians, and mixed-blood descendants of Europeans, Indians, and Africans—in colonial St. Louis. In 1787 there were about the same number of male and female slaves in St. Louis. Slaves performed much of the essential work for survival in the frontier community, including building, farming, and domestic work. They were entitled to food, clothing, and medical care and could not be killed or imprisoned without due process. Laws regulated work hours and prohibited sexual exploitation, but in practice slave women had no assurance that the slave codes would be enforced.

Music, dancing, and social events were important in St. Louis, as they were in other French settlements. The women commonly organized dances and parties. In the early years of the St. Louis settlement, community activities often crossed lines of culture, class, and race, but Corbett says that as merchant families "accumulated wealth and in-laws" they withdrew more into their own elite society.

Colonial St. Louis society blended social, legal, and cultural traditions in ways that often benefited women, particularly when compared with the way women were regarded in the Anglo-American colonies. This situation would change significantly for women who came into Missouri after the Louisiana Purchase.

Chapter 5

Journey to Missouri

ஃ

P reparing for the journey to America was a huge undertaking. There were countless decisions about which personal and household items were to be left behind and which were to be taken. Sometimes there was property to be sold. Special provisions had to be prepared or purchased for the long journey ahead.

Elise Dubach remembered that in the weeks leading up to her family's departure from Switzerland there was a new activity every night when she returned from school. One evening she came home to find her mother clarifying butter in a kettle on the stove. She boiled the butter until it became clear and then poured it into buckets to cool. Clarified butter would last indefinitely while salted butter would eventually turn rancid. Jeanette Dubach clarified twelve gallons of butter to be eaten on their voyage. She also packed cheese and dried fruit, including plums, cherries, and apples. The family packed their belongings in three large chests and disposed of what would not fit. Some of their best items were given to friends and relatives as keepsakes. Some surplus clothing was donated to the poor. Other items were sold at an auction that drew a large crowd.

The Dubachs left their farm and the village of Orvin in early February, as Uncle Christian had suggested, traveling first by wagon and then by train to the French port of Le Havre. When they

Irish immigrants leaving home. (State Historical Society of Missouri, Columbia)

arrived, their ship, the *Searampore*, was ready to depart as soon as the tide began to ebb. Benjamin hastily bought the remaining provisions they needed: crackers, potatoes, sugar, coffee, and lemons.

Most of the four hundred passengers, including the Dubachs, were crowded into the steerage section. As was the case with many immigrant ships, the *Searampore* carried cargo from America to Europe and returned filled with passengers. "The hold was arranged more for the herding of large numbers of people into small space than for comfort," Elise remembered. The berths were shelves ranged around the walls or built across the hold in tiers three bunks high. The ship provided mattresses, but the family used their own linen and blankets.

The ship also provided water, but the limited supply was carefully rationed, with only a small portion issued each day for adults and an even smaller portion for children. The water had to be used for drinking, cooking, and washing. Elise complained that there was never enough for all their needs, so they went without baths for two months.

Passengers provided their own food for the voyage. Elise remembered that the kitchens for passengers were located on the deck. They were covered but open on the sides. Each kitchen had a long iron trough in which the sailors built a fire. When the fire had burned down to coals, the passengers were called to cook their meals. Kettles were hung on an iron rod above the trough. One can imagine the scene as dozens of passengers crowded around to cook their meals at the same time over these fires.

Unlike most immigrants to Missouri, newlyweds Adelheid and Hermann Garlichs traveled to America in 1835 as privileged passengers. They encountered some rough weather early in the trip that brought on seasickness, and Adelheid also suffered from homesickness. At one point she wrote: "We are making good headway, but my thoughts are saddened when I remember that every wave dashing against the ship carries me farther away from my loved ones." Otherwise, the Garlichs couple seem to have had a pleasant journey. Their ship carried only 119 passengers. They had a private cabin and took their meals with the captain. They reported that the ship carried one hundred chickens, two pigs, two geese, and some ducks and pigeons to provide fresh meat for the journey. The young bride studied English, read, and discussed theological questions with her husband. Some days she knitted or did needlework while Pastor Garlichs entertained the other passengers with his violin. Henry Bode reported: "Often they tarried long on deck, discussing plans for the future, their simple home in the quiet backwoods, twenty-five miles beyond St. Charles." One of them recorded in their joint diary that the steerage passengers had given a theatrical program one day and that "it was very entertaining and they displayed some talent."

According to congressional testimony, 5,000 people left Antwerp for the United States in 1817, and 1,000 of them died en route. In an attempt to improve conditions on board the immigrant ships, Congress passed a law in 1819 limiting the number of passengers on a ship based on the ship's weight. In spite of this legislation, conditions on immigrant ships remained appalling. Captains were often paid on the basis of tonnage, so the more immigrants they could cram into the steerage sections, the more they earned. Lack of sanitation and ventilation below decks was a huge problem. There might be one chamber pot for fifty passengers, for example. Under these conditions, it is no wonder that illness was a constant threat. Typhus, cholera, smallpox, and dysentery were particularly common. Malnutrition was also common, and sometimes people starved to death. Spoilage, damage during storms, and long delays at sea might mean that food supplies were exhausted weeks before arrival.

In 1848 Congress again attempted to regulate immigrant ships and passed a law requiring sixteen square feet of space per person if the ceiling was less than six feet high and twenty-two square feet per person if the ceiling was less than five feet high. However, passengers had had more space under the passenger-tonnage ratio, and now shipowners scrambled to *downgrade* their facilities! The Bremen-based ship *Gallia* had previously carried 476 passengers; under the new law, it was refitted to carry 812. As a result, conditions worsened. In 1854, 1 out of every 6 passengers died or became seriously ill during the Atlantic voyage. That year one-fourth of the ships sailing from London arrived in North America with cases of cholera on board.

The large steamships that replaced sailing vessels later in the century were faster and safer, but conditions for steerage passengers were still bad. A passenger on a ship in 1906 reported that there were seven restrooms to be shared by 2,200 steerage passengers, five for men and two for women. He described a male lavatory as "exceedingly small and cramped" and said it was "simply packed, jammed to the doors, an hour before breakfast."

Elise Dubach remembered the death of a child after they had been at sea about ten days. A priest who was a passenger on the ship performed the service, and the child was buried at sea by the ship's crew. The body was weighted with iron and "the sailors comforted the parents with the assurance that the weight would haul the body so far beneath the surface that the sharks would never find it."

Many adults also died on the voyage. Franceska Lutz Riddle lost her husband during the Atlantic crossing. Franceska was born in Wiesloch in Baden in 1824. Her father was the mayor of the city, and her family was well-to-do. She married Frederick Riddle, a widower with a young daughter named Barbara. Frederick was also a government official but decided that America offered better opportunities for himself and his family. By the time they emigrated, Franceska had borne two sons, Mike and Jacob. Franceska's father gave her a gift of a small trunk of dried plums from his garden for the voyage. Their ship was driven off course, and the journey lasted sixty-six days. During the long voyage, Frederick became ill and died.

There were also many births on the ships. Doris Weatherford notes that many emigrants wanted to depart in the spring, and "to delay because of pregnancy would mean a whole year's wait, and by then one might be pregnant again." Jette Bruns reported a birth during her Atlantic crossing in 1836 aboard the *Ulysses*. She wrote to her brother Heinrich after arriving in Baltimore, describing the "long and arduous" voyage. She said that Clara Ossenbeck from Everswinkel was "happily delivered of a son" with Dr. Bruns (Jette's husband, Bernhard) in attendance. The child was named Johann Heinrich Bruno Ulysses and was baptized by the ship's chaplain. Captain J. H. Spilker and Jette were asked to serve as the child's godparents. Jette herself was in the early stages of her second pregnancy during the voyage.

America offered a new beginning to the immigrants who survived the difficult voyage, but for many the journey did not end with their arrival in a port city. Jette Bruns and other immigrants bound for Missouri still had a great distance to travel and more hardships to endure before reaching their destination. In the early years of settlement, new immigrants to Missouri came into seaports in the eastern United States and then traveled overland by wagons and boats to St. Louis.

Jette and Bernhard Bruns arrived in Baltimore on September 16. There they hired freight wagons to transport their goods. They traveled first to New York to meet a cousin and then went on to Philadelphia. "It was a wonderful trip, back on firm ground, traveling through beautiful country in a free nation," Jette reported. From Philadelphia they traveled by canal boats through the Allegheny Mountains. In Wheeling, Virginia, they waited a week for the wagons carrying their baggage to catch up with them. Next they trav-

Immigrants arriving at Castle Garden, New York. From 1855 until 1892, when Ellis Island became the point of entry for immigrants arriving in New York, millions were processed at Castle Garden. (State Historical Society of Missouri, Columbia)

eled down the Ohio River, but the river was low, and their river-boat ran onto a stump near Cincinnati. They continued their journey on a steamer called *Cavalier*, which took them to the Mississippi River and then upriver to St. Louis. There they boarded another steamer for the trip up the Missouri River to Jefferson City. From there they traveled up the Osage River on flatboats, finally arriving at their new home in Westphalia on November 2.

By the 1840s New Orleans had become the most popular seaport for immigrants on their way to Missouri. From there they traveled up the Mississippi on riverboats. When Elise Dubach and her family reached New Orleans in 1855 they immediately booked their passage on a steamboat to St. Louis. The boat was scheduled to leave two days later, but they were able to move aboard immediately and thus avoid the expense of hotel bills.

The Dubachs replenished their food supplies in New Orleans, buying large quantities of green vegetables and white bread, which they had missed on the long sea voyage. The trip to St. Louis took two weeks because they were on a slow boat "which stopped at nearly every town and plantation" between New Orleans and St. Louis. They did their own cooking on the steamboat as they had on the ship.

In St. Louis they boarded another steamboat heading up the Missouri River to St. Joseph. That leg of the journey took another week. In *Sunbonnet Days* Elise described what she called "the golden age" of steamboating in Missouri:

> Some of the boats had snow-white decks and the softest of Brussels carpeting for cabins and drawing rooms. Negroes who could sing were taken along for double service as deck hands and entertainers. The better boats carried pianos, and the more pretentious ones carried brass bands which blared upstream as they raced ahead of us. But passengers with a craving for luxury paid handsomely for it, a single fare from St. Louis to St. Joseph on a speedy packet being thirty dollars, which was as much as Father paid for his entire family on our slow boat. Our boat had no band, no piano, no negroes.

Nevertheless, Elise found her journey from St. Louis to St. Joseph an interesting experience. Watching the firemen stoke the furnace was fascinating, and she enjoyed the bustle of the boat pulling in to the riverbank for refueling. Farmers who lived along the river cut and stacked timber and left it on the bank ready to be loaded on the boats. The pilot sounded the boat's whistle to call the farmer to his woodpile, and he would arrive to collect his fee before the deckhands and working passengers had finished carrying the wood aboard.

Elise enjoyed the scenery along the Missouri better than that on the lower Mississippi, which had been somewhat monotonous. She described the excitement of passing through dangerous points on the Missouri River. "Every day I had occasion to hold my breath as the man at the wheel skillfully tempted the perils of that untamed river," she said. There were many dangers in the river: half-submerged trees, shifting sandbars, and deep channels that could undercut overhanging cliffs. The steamboat traveled day and night, although at night there was no illumination on the river except the glow from the furnaces. Elise said that the most skillful Missouri River pilots were paid as much as twelve hundred dollars a month, a "princely wage, especially in a day when a mechanic was lucky to draw one dollar a day."

She arrived in St. Joseph on May 6; she had traveled some three months. It is just as well that she was able to enjoy her trip up the Missouri River with such childlike joy and fascination. Less than two weeks after their arrival in St. Joseph, Elise would, as she put it, bury her childhood in the grave with her mother and become mother to her two younger brothers and housekeeper for her father. She was not quite thirteen years old.

Like Elise, many immigrant women began their new lives in America under difficult circumstances. After the death of her husband, Franceska Riddle continued to St. Louis, their planned destination. Shortly after she arrived she met Paul Andrew Hennerich, a widower, and made a marriage of convenience. Paul needed a wife and a mother for his son, Andrew, and Franceska needed a provider for herself, her two sons, and her stepdaughter.

After the Civil War immigrants typically traveled to Missouri by train, but the trains were overcrowded, and the journey could still be arduous. The journey of Italian immigrant Rosa Cassettari and her companions, traveling to Missouri in 1884, was made more difficult because an Italian man pretending to befriend them cheated them in New York. The fact that he spoke Italian inspired their confidence. He put them up in a hotel, telling them they would have to wait three days for a train to Missouri, when in fact there were two every day. He eventually put them on a train to Missouri, but he took all their money first. "He left us not even a crust of bread for our journey. And we didn't even guess that he was fooling us," she said. Rosa and her friends traveled all the way from New York to Missouri with nothing to eat.

Immigrants endured seasickness, homesickness, lack of space and privacy, and shortages of water and food all for the sake of a better life in America. No doubt they hoped for a friendly welcome upon arrival and acceptance into their new communities. Unfortunately, there were new perils to face in the New World. They might have been wary of being taken advantage of by American landlords and bosses, but they did not expect to be cheated by their own countrymen. They had much to learn and many hardships to overcome.

Chapter 6

Life in Early St. Louis

୬ୄଡ଼ୄଡ଼ଡ଼

B ecause of its location at the confluence of the Mississippi
and Missouri Rivers, St. Louis was well situated to become
a center for shipping and commerce for the nation's west-
ward expansion. Although most of the new settlers coming into the
Missouri Territory in the early nineteenth century were American,
new European immigrants also helped shape the city of St. Louis.
The life of Rose Philippine Duchesne provides a story of one remark-
able immigrant woman's labor in early St. Louis. Her work in the
growing city spanned more than three tumultuous decades, from
1818 to 1852.

She was born into a wealthy family in Grenoble, France, in 1769.
Her father was a lawyer. Like many girls from well-to-do families,
she was sent to boarding school. While at the Order of the Visitation convent school she decided to pursue a religious vocation. Her
parents were unhappy with this decision and withdrew her from the
school to distance her from the influence of the nuns. However, to
avoid an unwanted marriage, she defied her parents and entered
the convent as a novice at the age of eighteen. During the French
Revolution, the sisters, along with nearly all religious orders in
France, were disbanded. She returned to her family and spent the
next decade devoting herself to charitable work.

Eventually, Sister Duchesne was able to resume her religious life,

View of St. Louis from the Illinois side of the Mississippi River. (A. E. Schroeder Collection)

and she joined a new order—the Religious of the Sacred Heart of Jesus. She was a convent school administrator when Louis William Valentine DuBourg, bishop of Louisiana, visited Paris to raise money and recruit missionaries for his frontier diocese in America.

In 1818, at the age of forty-nine, Mother Duchesne was chosen to lead a group of nuns who were being sent to the frontier city of St. Louis to found a convent and a school. She felt this would allow her to fulfill a lifelong ambition to be a missionary to the Indians in America. The party of five set sail in March on the American ship *Rebecca*. The journey took seventy days. During the voyage they endured storms, an encounter with pirates, a fire on deck, seasickness, and moldy biscuits. Mother Duchesne was forced to spend a period of convalescence at an Ursuline convent in New Orleans before continuing on to St. Louis. The steamboat journey up the Mississippi took another forty days, including nineteen hours aground on a sandbar. The nuns arrived in St. Louis on August 21.

Bishop DuBourg sent them to the town of St. Charles, a day's travel west from St. Louis on the far side of the Missouri River, to open a boarding school. There they founded the first convent of the Religious of the Sacred Heart of Jesus in America. In September 1818 they opened the first free school for girls west of the Mississippi. Shortly after, they added a boarding school. The girls were to be taught religion, reading, writing, and arithmetic. After some persuasion, the bishop allowed the nuns to teach black girls one day a week. However, few girls enrolled in the school, and it was soon clear that the boarding school, which was to be the main source of revenue for the convent, would not succeed in St. Charles.

Conditions were very difficult for the nuns that first year. In December, Mother Duchesne wrote to the mother house in France: "We have had the privilege of doing without bread and water. . . . The Missouri is almost frozen over, and it is so cold that the water freezes beside the fire. . . . We have logs, but they are too large, and there is no one to chop them for us and no saw with which we might cut them ourselves." She was disappointed not to be working with Indians, but in February 1819 she wrote:

> If our sisters in France imagine us to be surrounded by savages, they are quite mistaken. . . . But to compensate for our disappointment we have new employments: we dig in the garden, carry out the manure, water the cow, clean out her little stable. . . . And we do all this with as much joy as we would have if we were teaching Indians, for God wills it this way, and our poverty . . . prevents us from getting servants.

In September 1819 the convent was moved to Florissant, which was closer to St. Louis. Regarding the move, Mother Duchesne wrote that the cows were "indignant at being tied, and the sisters were forced to coax them the entire distance with cabbages." She "divided [her] attention between the reliquaries and the hens."

An 1824 letter described some of their household work at the Florissant convent: "We make our soap, candles for both the house and the church, altar-breads, our butter, woolen yarn, and cotton and linen thread." They had sown cotton seeds that year, but the seeds were not suited to the local climate. Mother Duchesne wrote that she hoped to buy a loom for weaving cloth and noted that they knew how to dye cloth in black, gray, and yellow by making dye from native plants. Their food supply consisted of salt pork, milk, and vegetables from their garden. At that time the school offered English, grammar, writing, arithmetic, history, geography, and sewing and embroidery.

In 1826 Irishman John Mullanphy offered the order eighty acres and a small house in St. Louis on the condition that they accept 20 orphans of his choice each year as charity boarding students. However, he insisted that the girls not be allowed to wear shoes or drink imported beverages "lest they be trained above the station in life which fate had set for them." The order opened the first orphanage in St. Louis. The work of the order grew, and a decade after she arrived in the St. Louis area Mother Duchesne administered six schools for girls, including three in the St. Louis area, which served more than 350 students.

The schools and other services were needed because St. Louis began to experience a period of rapid growth in the 1830s. Many of the newcomers to the city were immigrants from Europe, particularly the German states and Ireland. A number of Irish immigrants were firmly entrenched in St. Louis life and politics by the 1830s. Many of the early Irish settlers were prosperous and accepted as part of the city's elite society. Probably the most famous was Mother Duchesne's benefactor, John Mullanphy, who had come to St. Louis from Ireland in 1804 and opened a store. He had made a fortune through several lucrative ventures, including selling cotton at the end of the War of 1812. He was said to be the richest man in the Mississippi valley at the time of his death, and he left his surviving children wealthy. His daughter Anne Mullanphy Biddle donated much of her wealth to Catholic charitable institutions serving women and children.

When Fredrick Steines and his wife and four children arrived in St. Louis in 1834, there were about eighteen German families and a few unmarried Germans among the city's seven thousand residents. Steines had been a teacher in Prussia and led the Solingen

Emigration Society to Missouri in search of political freedom. The Steines family arrived in St. Louis in July, but within a week Fredrick's wife and four children had all died of cholera. His sister-in-law also died. Whatever hopes these two women had for their lives in the New World, they remained unfulfilled. After the deaths of his wife and children, Steines moved to Franklin County and opened a school for boys.

St. Louis's rapid population growth created enormous problems. Thousands of travelers and new immigrants reached the city each month. Sometimes the city's population grew by more than 10 percent in just a few days. On a single day in 1844, there were more than fifteen hundred new arrivals. New buildings were being built at a phenomenal rate, but there was never enough housing available.

Poor sanitation and crowded living conditions made St. Louis one of the unhealthiest cities in the world. Epidemics of smallpox, influenza, cholera, and other diseases were common. A cholera epidemic in 1832 killed 5 percent of the population. There was another epidemic the following year. The city's systems for dealing with garbage and sewage were completely inadequate. Dead animals were frequently left in the streets to rot. When the Saxons arrived in the city in 1839, many became ill because of the change in climate, crowded housing, and exposure to unsanitary conditions. Historian Walter Forster estimates that sixty-five or seventy of the group of about six hundred died within three or four months of their arrival in St. Louis.

The annual death rate for the 1840s was approximately one in twenty-three. By comparison, the rate was one in fifty-four in New Orleans and one in forty-four in Boston. Twenty-five percent of the children born in St. Louis during this period died before they were a year old; 40 percent died before their fifth birthday. In late December 1848 a steamboat arrived in St. Louis with thirty cholera victims among the passengers and crew. The cholera epidemic that resulted killed almost a tenth of the city's population. In all social classes, women had the primary responsibility for providing care for the sick and comforting the survivors.

Many who died left behind orphaned children. Well-to-do women responded to the need for social services by setting up charitable organizations to provide homes for orphans and shelters for the sick and dependent, particularly women. In addition to paying dues and raising money in the community, women provided support in other ways, such as sewing clothes for orphaned children.

By 1850, the population of St. Louis had grown to nearly 78,000 people. More than half of the people in the city at that time had lived there less than two years, and there were more foreign-born than native-born residents. German immigrants—24,000 in 1850, and 50,000 by 1860—were the largest foreign-born group in the city. Many of the Germans who had come into St. Louis had savings or cash from selling property in Germany. In the early 1850s, Germans owned one-third of all new businesses in St. Louis. German men had skills that were in demand in the rapidly growing city. They worked as blacksmiths, barbers, shoemakers, stonemasons, carpenters, brewers, and in many other trades. German businesses, social clubs, and music and theater groups thrived. German-language newspapers were published in the city. New German neighborhoods formed on the northern and southern edges of the city and farther out in the county. Many German women had little direct contact with American culture, because they conducted all their business within a few blocks of their homes and never needed to speak English.

Irish immigrants, on the other hand, generally arrived in St. Louis with few skills beyond farming and little or no money. More than 30,000 came to St. Louis between 1830 and 1860. Many lived in crowded buildings on the city's north side. In 1842 a group of Irish settlers moved to an open section of ground northwest of the city limits and took up illegal residence there. They built small makeshift shanties arranged in no particular pattern. Fortunately for the settlers, the land was owned by John Mullanphy's heirs, who chose to ignore the squatters. The area, known as Kerry Patch, became the center of St. Louis's Irish community.

The Irish in St. Louis worked in a wide variety of jobs, mostly as manual laborers. Historian William Faherty notes, for example, that a dozen Irish gardeners planted trees and trimmed hedges on the Henry Shaw estate, which would later become the Missouri Botanical Garden. There were many opportunities for work in the growing St. Louis economy in flour mills, sawmills, foundries, and manufacturing plants. The constant traffic on the rivers created jobs for steamboat hands and dockworkers.

Although anti-immigrant feelings in St. Louis never reached the extreme levels they did in some other American cities, the huge influx of immigrants in these decades did create tensions. Conflicts arose over various issues, including religion, alcohol, and public social gatherings on Sundays. In the late 1830s there was an active anti-Catholic press stirring up hostility toward Catholic immigrants. Some Protestant leaders opposed these actions, but others did not, worried that Catholics would be influenced by the Church's negative attitude toward democratic values. Not all anti-Catholicism came from Americans. Some of the most vigorous attacks on the Catholic Church came from the German Freethinkers in St. Louis, who were strongly anticlerical. There was a brief flurry of anti-Catholic sentiment in the city again in the 1840s, culminating when rioters broke into the St. Louis University School of Medicine in 1844 and destroyed equipment.

The Americans also targeted Germans. One source of tension was the common German practice of spending Sunday afternoons at beer gardens, theaters, or music halls. Many Americans believed such social activities were inappropriate on the Sabbath. When anti-immigrant politicians took control of city government briefly in the 1840s, they attempted to prevent these social gatherings by cutting off public transportation on Sunday afternoons.

Anti-immigrant feelings continued to run high in the 1850s. Rioting broke out again in 1852 when shops and houses belonging to Irish families were damaged on the city's north side and again on election day in 1854 in the heavily Irish Fifth Ward. Washington King, a candidate of the anti-immigrant Know-Nothing Party, was elected mayor in 1855. This time anti-immigrant forces were more successful in hindering immigrants' Sunday activities. Instead of a ban on public transportation, they imposed Sunday closing laws

Mother Rose Philippine Duchesne. (State Historical Society of Missouri, Columbia)

that they enforced against Irish and German pubs, beer gardens, and theaters that sold alcohol. Such hostile actions certainly affected the lives of many of the city's immigrant women.

Not much is known about the lives of ordinary immigrant women during this period. Most married women were not employed, although some worked in family-run businesses such as stores or taverns. Some were seamstresses or milliners. Many Irish women earned money doing laundry, sewing, and taking in lodgers.

A few unmarried women worked in the garment industry, but far more found work in domestic service. Most women employed outside their homes did cooking, cleaning, and laundry for others, frequently in boardinghouses. Katharine Corbett says that one in three St. Louisans lived in boardinghouses in 1850, and nearly half of the Irish lived in rented rooms. In the mid-1850s St. John the Evangelist Catholic Church held a service at five o'clock in the morning so that young Irish women in domestic service could attend mass and return to work in time to fix breakfast for their employers. Unlike cities in the eastern United States that had industrialized earlier, St. Louis did not have factories employing many women at this time. In 1860, there were only 814 women employed by St. Louis manufacturers.

Rose Philippine Duchesne died in St. Charles in 1852 at the age of eighty-two. She had devoted much of her life's labor to the education of women, first in her native France and then in frontier Missouri. She and other immigrants transformed a small frontier town into a dynamic, booming city. St. Louis experienced rapid growth and change during Duchesne's lifetime, but there were more changes to come. Both the makeup of the immigrant population in the city and the nature of women's work would change dramatically by the end of the century.

Chapter 7

Immigrant Women on the Frontier

॰॰॰॰॰

W omen on the frontier faced similar conditions, shared common experiences, and did much the same kind of work whether they were foreign-born or settlers from eastern states. Immigrant women had to learn how to deal with new situations, new materials, and new foods, such as cooking over an open fire and making bread from cornmeal. Linda Pickle says that "self-reliant, subsistence farming in the early years of settlement, without the support of the Old World village, meant a reversion to old methods of food and clothing production for many women."

Frontier homes in Missouri were usually primitive log cabins. This could be very disheartening for women who were accustomed to nicer homes in Europe. Not long after her arrival in Westphalia, Jette Bruns wrote to her brother Heinrich: "When it rains, it is just too sad in these log cabins. . . . In cold weather one is a little hesitant to get up in the morning, and I frequently think back to our comfortable living room. However, here we just have to live through it." Women of the poorer classes who had lived in miserable conditions in Europe probably found frontier conditions less shocking and thus easier to endure.

Women helped with the most difficult frontier tasks, including clearing forests, removing tree stumps, splitting logs for fences, and

PIONEER LIFE IN MISSOURI IN 1820.

Missouri's early settlers often lived in log houses. Although this scene is somewhat idealized, it illustrates the variety of activities that were part of family life on the frontier. (State Historical Society of Missouri, Columbia)

building houses. In the 1830s Margaret Blauff Hillenkamp, in between bearing several children, helped her husband clear forty acres of forested land in St. Charles County for crops and a peach and apple orchard. More-typical work for frontierswomen included planting gardens, preserving food, milking cows, and tending chickens, sheep, pigs, and other animals. These chores were in addition to household duties such as cooking, churning butter, cleaning, doing laundry, and sewing. Women bore many children and frequently carried out their duties while pregnant or nursing. Caring for children of various ages was a constant part of a mother's life. Women in areas where there were no schools sometimes taught their children to read and write.

Frontier women also assisted with seasonal chores such as raking hay, harvesting grain, gathering firewood, and butchering. Other

Jette Bruns's 1850 sketch (redrawn by Frank Stack) of the half-timbered house she and Dr. Bruns built in Westphalia in 1836–1838. It was quite lavish compared to their first home, a simple log cabin with a window. (Carla Schulz-Geisberg Collection, courtesy of A. E. Schroeder)

tasks might include carding and spinning wool, weaving and dying cloth, and knitting or doing needlework. Access to water was a major concern for all settlers on the frontier, and carrying water was often one of a woman's most onerous chores. Pickle notes that, in general, adjusting to frontier life was easier for settlers in Missouri, Illinois and Iowa than for those on the Great Plains, in part because of the availability of water.

Maxine Schwartz Seller notes that European immigrant women who had been accustomed to "the companionship of friends and relatives and the sociability of village life" were dismayed to find themselves on homesteads many miles from their nearest neighbors. Sometimes women were called on to assist neighbors. As they did everywhere, women often served as midwives, cared for the sick, and prepared the dead for burial. Unfortunately, help was not always available, and as Seller points out, isolation could be fatal in times of injury, illness, or a difficult childbirth.

One aspect of their lives that set immigrant women apart from their American counterparts on the frontier was language. Because women in isolated areas had few contacts outside their homes or immediate neighborhoods, many did not learn to speak English well—if at all. Men were more likely to travel into nearby settlements to buy supplies, but a woman on a frontier homestead might go weeks or even months without seeing anyone outside her immediate family.

Elise Dubach's father, Benjamin, bought 160 acres of land "a day's ox-team drive" northwest of St. Joseph. The claim was mostly upland prairie, but about 60 acres was timbered bottomland along the Missouri River, opposite the Missouri town of Amazonia. There was a one-room log cabin and a stone quarry on the farm.

Benjamin bought the basic furniture they needed to supplement the feather beds and other household furnishings they had brought from Switzerland. He also purchased a plow and other farm tools, cows, four oxen, and a saddle pony. Equipping the family for farming and housekeeping used up most of his money, but there was enough left to buy lumber and other materials to floor the cabin and the sleeping loft and put in a window. He also rechinked the walls to make them tight against wind, rain, and snow, and he dug a well.

In *Sunbonnet Days,* Elise describes how her father and brothers broke the prairie sod, and how they worked from dawn to dark through the summer putting in crops, hoeing the corn, and finally gathering in the harvest. Benjamin planted a vegetable garden near the house that yielded a bountiful harvest of potatoes and other vegetables. In the winter the Dubachs had fresh pork and beef to eat. In the summer they ate chicken, dried beef, salt pork, and hams, bacon, and sausage, which they had cured in their smokehouse.

Elise took butter and eggs to sell in nearby Amazonia and brought home dry goods and groceries from McChesner's General Store. She crossed the Missouri River by boat in the summer and by horseback when it was frozen solid in the winter. During parts of the spring and fall the river was impassable, and the Dubachs had to make their supplies last until they could cross over again. Besides what Elise sold in town, in the winter Benjamin cut firewood to sell to steamboats in the summer. He also raised oxen to sell in St. Joseph. He received top prices for his oxen, which were in great demand by the many settlers heading west.

Although Elise was thirteen when she, her father, and her two younger brothers moved into their log cabin, she managed the household. She cooked, cleaned, sewed, did the laundry, helped in the garden, and made butter, cheese, soap, and candles. The family sewing took a good deal of Elise's time. Not only did she mend everyone's clothes, but she made dresses and sunbonnets for herself, jackets and trousers for her brothers, and shirts for her father. She learned how to make clothing from her neighbor, a Mrs. Boston, who lived half a mile away.

Candlelight was the only illumination the Dubachs had on their prairie farm. Candles were made from a small amount of beeswax and tallow rendered from beef fat, and Elise made hundreds of candles in the winter after the family had butchered. Elise could cast eight candles at a time in her mold. She hung a string of wicking in each candle form, melted tallow and wax together, and poured the mixture into the mold. She hung the mold to cool overnight and removed the candles in the morning. She repeated the process each day until all the tallow was made into candles.

Laundry soap was another by-product of butchering. In the fall her father killed a hog to provide meat and lard for the winter. Part of the lard was used for cooking, but the rest was mixed with lye to make soap. Elise made lye from the wood ashes she saved from the kitchen stove each day. The ashes were kept in a wooden hopper her father had made. When it was full, she poured water over them to leach out the lye, which then dripped into a crock. The lye was left to stand in the sun to become concentrated as the water evaporated. To make soap, she boiled hog fat in a sixteen-gallon iron kettle hung over a fire in the backyard. When the fat was clear, she stirred liquid lye into the boiling fat. This mixture was kept boiling most of a day, and the soap was salted to cause excess lye to sink to the bottom. Then she allowed the fire to die down. As the kettle cooled, the soap hardened. Finally, Elise cut the soap into cakes, which she wrapped in paper and stored in boxes. Usually she made enough soap at one time to last a year.

Elise also made cheese, as she had watched her mother do in Switzerland. Before they left home, her Uncle Christian had written to say that there was no cheese available in St. Joseph, nor any rennet, the ingredient needed to curdle milk in the cheesemaking process. When they were preparing for the journey to America, they had packed twenty calf stomachs to provide rennet. In St. Joseph, Elise taught her Aunt Christine how to make cheese, and later she also taught many of her frontier neighbors.

Elise kept house for her father and brothers on the Kansas farm for three years. When her father married again, her Uncle Christian and Aunt Christine invited her to live with them in St. Joseph. They believed that "a girl who had been the manager of a home for three years might not yield readily to the rule of a stepmother." She accepted this invitation and later thought it had been a good decision. She was glad she had the opportunity to complete her Americanization in the bustling city of St. Joseph.

Chapter 8

German Women and the Church

⚘

T here were few opportunities on the frontier for women to
see other women outside their immediate families except
for Sunday church services. In small immigrant towns
throughout the state, the church was nearly always the heart of the
community. Women in Missouri's German communities rarely took
a visible, public role in church life, but Linda Pickle says immigrant
churches "could not have functioned or, sometimes, survived without the on-going work women performed." In Missouri's early history, women fed and housed traveling ministers, kept the church
clean, decorated the altar for Sunday services, and held various
fund-raisers. The wives of rural ministers often shouldered the hard
physical labor of farm work with little or no help from their husbands, who were away from home much of the time because they
traveled long distances as they served the needs of several parishes.

Adelheid von Borries, only eighteen when she married Pastor
Hermann Garlichs in 1835, was the first German Evangelical minister's wife in the Missouri wilderness. Adelheid was born into an
aristocratic family and grew up with the comforts of a wealthy home.
Her father, Philip C. L. von Borries, was the head of an administra-
tive district in Prussia. Henry Bode, who wrote a colorful chronicle
of the lives of the Garlichs couple in *Builders of Our Foundations*,
said: "What a contrast between the mansion she left behind and

their first abode in America, an old one-room log shack on a lone farm, where wintry blasts drove snow through the crevices, and where in summer snakes wriggled through the cracks, their tongues hissing ugly warnings." They lived in the log cabin a year and a half—a hardship "sweetened only by the bliss of newlyweds" according to Bode—before moving into a parsonage in the fall of 1837. The new house contained two large rooms on the ground floor with sleeping quarters above. Adelheid gave birth to six children in Missouri, three boys and three girls.

In the early years Pastor Garlichs's ministry in the Femme Osage Valley included five separate congregations. Bode reported that the pastor's wife was "a good hearted person" but had a temper that flared up at times. Two young assistant pastors stayed with the family from 1844 to 1846, and it was their responsibility to chop firewood. When the sticks were too long and kept the stove door from closing, the room filled with smoke. Bode, who granted that this would have been "vexing to any housewife," said Adelheid always lost her temper on such occasions. "But," he added, "when it was over she was again her cheerful self, amiable and lovely, and no one could harbor any grudge against her." Adelheid and her family left Missouri in 1846 because of the lack of income and her husband's poor health. His combined income at that time was less than two hundred dollars a year from all the congregations, and not all of that was paid in cash. He said in his memoirs, "For the most part I had to take it in produce, corn, butter, etc., usually much below the amount due me."

The Garlichs family went back to Germany, where Hermann rested and recovered his health. When they returned to America, he took a position in Brooklyn, New York. Adelheid had eleven children in all, two of whom died in infancy. Hermann died in 1865, leaving her with seven children still at home and without means, according to Bode. He did not explain how she managed her affairs as a widow, saying only that she did not fear for the future, knowing that she could rely on her "children's love and respect." She and three daughters returned to Germany again in 1870, and she died there the following year.

In Protestant German churches, women were not generally allowed to serve directly. In early Missouri Synod Lutheran communities women were not even allowed to teach school, although this prohibition was gradually relaxed because of a shortage of male teachers for the Lutheran schools. Julie Turnau from Hannover wanted to do missionary work in Africa for the German Evangelical Church, but the missionary societies would not take single women, so she decided to marry a missionary. In 1842 she sailed to America to marry a man she had never met, George Wall. He was the founder of Holy Ghost Church, the first German Protestant congregation in St. Louis. Julie traveled with a newly married missionary couple also going to St. Louis, Louis Nollau and his wife. She wrote in her diary that she hoped to provide her husband more time for his pastoral work by making his domestic life easier. "I am happy that I shall be able to be active in God's work through such ordinary housework, if not directly, at any rate indirectly." George Wall established five more Evangelical congregations in St. Louis. Julie bore nine children, six of whom were still living when her husband died twenty-five years after their marriage. A printed memorial to George Wall, now in the Eden Theological Seminary Archives, commended Julie as well: "In her the Lord gave him a true life-companion on the way to the heavenly fatherland, participating fully with him in domestic and churchly joys and sorrows."

Most immigrant women came to Missouri as part of family units, but some, particularly Germans, came as part of organized groups or settlement societies. Living within structured groups certainly affected women's experiences in America. Not all of these groups were overtly religious, but there are several notable examples of religious settlements in the state.

One of the largest settlement groups, and one that had a significant and lasting impact, was the Saxon Lutherans, who came to Missouri under the leadership of Martin Stephan in the late 1830s. Stephan, the controversial but popular pastor of St. John's Church in Dresden, formed an emigration society when he found himself in trouble with the civil and religious authorities there. Several hundred people pooled their money and agreed to follow him to Mis-

Reverend Henry and Mrs. Hulda Nagel and family. Caroline Emilie Hulda Meusch was the daughter of the president of the proseminary in Illinois (later Elmhurst College), which prepared students for Eden Seminary. Henry fell in love with Hulda while he was a student at the college. They were married in 1893. (Courtesy of Paul C. Nagel)

souri, where he planned to build an autonomous religious community in the wilderness, one that could function without the interference of king's officers or a church hierarchy. One of the five ships chartered for the venture was lost at sea with some sixty passengers, a large sum of money, and valuable possessions. The first group to arrive in Missouri included more than six hundred immigrants, and nearly half of them were female. Most of the women were home-makers, but there were also twenty-two maids, three midwives, and four seamstresses. Linda Pickle notes that, for the women who came with this group, "their conviction that they were taking part in a God-willed endeavor fortified them, at least in part, for the hard-ships ahead." Life was difficult in both overcrowded St. Louis and in the primitive Perry County settlements.

In the early years in Perry County, according to Walter Forster, author of *Zion on the Mississippi,* "starvation was averted for some of the German colonists only by the generous hospitality and frontier neighborliness of the English, Scotch, Irish, and French in the southeastern Missouri area." The Saxon immigrants were not ade-quately prepared for their move to the wilderness of southeast Missouri in 1839. In part because of Stephan's extravagant spend-ing in St. Louis, the colonists did not have the resources to buy livestock or farm equipment. The lack of draft animals meant that the settlers had to do even the heaviest work, such as hauling logs for their cabins, themselves. They were inefficient, inept builders. The first spring, according to Forster, "almost all of the men and some women and children slept in shacks, or lean-tos, or out in the open. . . . Both the emigrants and their possessions were frequently drenched by seasonal spring rains." The group ran out of money for food. Summer brought unaccustomed heat and fevers of various descriptions. Forster reports that "a tragically large number of the settlers died, sometimes for want of proper care or because of fail-ure to take the necessary precautions."

In the fall of 1839, Christiane Loeber, the unmarried sister of Pastor G. H. Loeber, reported in a letter that her American neigh-bors had had a productive year:

> This disposes these people, who are mostly very good people anyway, so kindly toward us that they aid us in many ways with victuals and other assistance. They give our people large wag-onfuls of apples and sacks of flour, and one may stay with them as long as one likes to gather supplies for the winter; as I have

already done on two occasions; when, it is true, I reciprocated by doing some knitting and sewing for them, by which one does them a great favor, but for which one is nevertheless amply rewarded.

Despite this help, the new immigrants still struggled to survive. In particular, illness remained a constant threat. Christiane Loeber herself became ill in April 1840 and died two days later. Forster says general conditions did not improve in the communities until the fall of 1841.

A detailed set of codes had been prepared before the settlement group left Saxony, covering a confession of faith, various points about the emigration and its purpose and structure, the credit fund, travel to America, regulations for settlement, and regulations for the civil community. Some of the regulations applied specifically to the women in the group. The travel regulations included provisions for supervision of the women and children on board ship and even specified what their conduct should be in the event that a storm should strike on the Atlantic crossing: "They are to call upon God for gracious deliverance, as befits Christians, and avoid as much as possible that disturbance and confusion should result from their outcries and running about." The police ordinances prohibited theaters, dance halls, games of chance, and cursing and also regulated clothing: "All clothing which is injurious to health and is against Christian decency is forbidden. Corsets and their equivalents, such as dresses stiffened in the upper part with whalebone, are entirely forbidden to the women, as especially harmful to their health." Penalties for transgressions were to be public and could include admonition, fines, and possibly, expulsion from the community.

Four Buenger sisters—Emilie, Agnes, Lydia, and Clementine— came to Missouri as part of this group. Their father and grandfather were Lutheran pastors. An account written by one of Clementine's descendants says that another sister, "little Emma," was left behind in Germany because of her delicate health and was adopted by a family friend. Clementine was seventeen when she came to Missouri. She married Gottlob J. Neumueller a year later. He made a

Conrad Finck and his children, ca. 1862. Notice the absence of Beatrice Finck, who died in 1859, leaving behind five young children. (From Henry T. Finck, *My Adventures in the Golden Age of Music*)

meager living digging cellars and cisterns in the summer and mending shoes in the winter. They had eleven children, seven of whom survived their mother.

Emilie, Agnes, and Lydia all married Lutheran ministers who would be important in the development of the Missouri Synod Lutheran Church. Lydia married Pastor J. F. K. Lochner. The newlyweds moved into a one-room cabin at Pleasant Ridge in 1847. Pickle reports that Lydia "wept upon seeing the cabin and had to get into bed under an umbrella to shelter herself from the snow drifting through the faulty roof." A year and a half later, she died a month after giving birth for the first time. She had contracted an illness when spring rains flooded the cabin. Emilie married C. F. W. Walther, who became the first president of the Evangelical Lutheran Synod of Missouri, Ohio, and Other States when it was founded in 1847. Agnes married Walther's older brother, Otto, who was the first pastor of the St. Louis Trinity congregation. After his death in 1841, she married another minister, Otto Fuerbringer, and went with him to a frontier church in Michigan.

Bethel, in Shelby County in northeast Missouri, was founded as a religious commune in 1844. The leader, Wilhelm Keil, rejected established Christian denominations and drew a large number of followers in Pennsylvania, Ohio, and other states. He led a group west to Missouri to form a community based on his understanding of the Bible, promising nothing but bread, water, and hard work. In the Bethel colony, property was held in common, and work was shared by the community. The church stressed a practical Christianity based on the ideals of equality and sharing. The community offered shelter, food, and medical care to anyone who agreed to live by its principles. People worked as they were able, and no records or accounts of an individual's labor were kept. Unmarried women in Bethel often worked in community enterprises, such as the glove factory. A visitor to Bethel reported that every house had a garden with vegetables and flowers. Each family had cows, pigs, and poultry to provide milk, butter, meat, and eggs. Families could trade extra domestic products at the community store for items they could not produce themselves. Beatrice Finck, who was married to Conrad Finck, a pharmacist and music teacher, described her daily life in Bethel in a letter to her relatives in Germany:

> Besides attending to the things my dear mother taught me, such as cooking, baking, washing, ironing, sewing, knitting, mending, etc. . . . Well, I can milk a cow, which gives me great pleasure; also I can make trousers, vests and coats. There is no work I dodge and I am not ashamed to perform the humblest tasks. . . . I often sing from morn to night.

After the Civil War a group of German Baptists from Virginia, called Dunkards, founded Rockingham in Ray County. These settlers were not first-generation immigrants, but they had maintained their language and their cultural identity. Farms in the settlement were individually owned, but much of the seasonal work was done by the community as a whole. The men joined together in harvesting crops, threshing, butchering, and building. The women shared the work of cooking for community gatherings, canning, and quilting. James M. Shirky, the great-grandson of community founders Samuel and Catharine Shirky, reported that a Dunkard meal required a great amount of work "by way of the garden, the berry patch, the smokehouse, the milkhouse, the cellar, the chicken house, the barn and the pantry."

The Dunkard church embraced a doctrine of simplicity to be manifested in "plain living, plain dress, plain food and temperance." Behavior in the community was strictly regulated. A committee of church elders visited all church members before the Love Feast held in the spring and fall "to ascertain that there was no ill will or feuding, no unpaid bills, nor any wayward behavior" as Shirky explained. Another kind of visitation occurred when emissaries from the church were sent by the church council to see those who were to be admonished or otherwise punished for offensive behavior. In November 1882, for example, a complaint was heard against a Sister Rebecca "for adorning herself in immodest apparel and wearing a breast pin." In December, after church representatives visited her, the church council took up her case and expelled her from the church. In 1895, the two brethren who visited a woman named Etta reported that she "says she has been to a dance, has banged her hair, is wearing a hat, etc. and expects to continue this way." She was disowned, considered a more serious penalty than being expelled. The church dropped this kind of inquisition around the turn of the century.

Women's lives were different in each of these three religious communities, but their hard work and dedication were important to the daily functioning of the community and the church. Pickle says of the women of the Saxon immigration, "Almost anonymous as individuals, they were collectively a necessary part of the foundation on which the edifice of their community, their church, was built." The same could be said of the women in other churches.

Chapter 9

Immigrant Women in Religious Orders

৯৽৽৽

No history of immigrant women in Missouri would be complete without a discussion of the foreign-born nuns who served in religious orders in the state. Rose Philippine Duchesne was one of the first missionary nuns to come to Missouri, but many others followed in her footsteps. These women educated the children of immigrants and Americans, cared for the sick and homeless, and performed many other acts of charity. They suffered the same hardships and deprivations as other settlers, including illness and, sometimes, early death. William Faherty notes that two Sisters of Charity, three Sisters of Saint Joseph, one Visitandine, and six Religious of the Sacred Heart died during the St. Louis cholera epidemic of 1849, most of them while caring for the sick.

Joseph Rosati was appointed bishop of St. Louis in 1827. At the time of his appointment, the diocese included the western half of Illinois and all American territory west of the Mississippi and north of the state of Louisiana. It was roughly the size of the other nine dioceses in the United States combined. Obviously, he needed help to meet the needs of his parishioners in this vast region.

The Sisters of Charity in Emmitsburg, Maryland, sent a mission to St. Louis in 1828 to found the Mullanphy Hospital. This order later merged with the Daughters of Charity of St. Vincent de Paul. As the immigrant population of St. Louis grew, the Daughters of

Charity, many of whom were themselves immigrants, provided care for women and children in need. Few recent immigrants had extended families in the area to provide care in times of need during this period. The Daughters of Charity ran orphanages, schools for girls, homes for elderly widows, maternity hospitals, and an institute for the mentally ill.

In the mid-1830s Bishop Rosati wrote to Mother St. John Fontbonne, superior of the Sisters of St. Joseph in Lyon, France, requesting that she send a few members of her community to St. Louis to start a school for the deaf. The order, founded in 1693, had operated schools and charitable institutions in France until the French Revolution. Many of the sisters had been imprisoned during the Reign of Terror. In 1807 Mother St. John Fontbonne had gathered a few remaining members of the community and revived the order, which eventually reopened more than two hundred schools, orphanages, and hospitals in France.

The Countess de la Roche-Jacqueline, an admirer of Mother St. John's and friend of the order, agreed to fund this mission "to convert the savages, to teach their children and those of the Protestant families." Six nuns, including two nieces of Mother St. John, were chosen for the mission to Missouri. The sisters boarded the *Heidelberg* in Le Havre to cross the Atlantic in January 1836. The oldest member of the group was thirty-one, the youngest twenty-one. Two other sisters began their training to learn to teach the deaf. They would join the group when their training was complete.

After the six nuns reached St. Louis in late March, three of them went to the swampy but generally prosperous farming community of Cahokia, Illinois. The villagers had built a two-story frame house for them, and a large crowd turned out to greet them the day they arrived. A few days later they opened a school for thirty students. The Sisters of St. Joseph maintained a community in Cahokia until 1855, although it was eventually closed because the low-lying village flooded frequently and illness was common.

The other three nuns were sent to the Missouri village of Carondelet. The people in Carondelet were poor and made their living mainly from cutting wood. The village had been known locally as "*Vide Poche*" or "Empty Pockets." Faherty says the people of Carondelet "showed little interest in either religion or education." The local priest, Father Edmund Saulnier, told the sisters that he was unable to help them; they would have to visit the families in the village to ask for food. The three nuns moved into a two-room log cabin being vacated by the Sisters of Charity, who were moving their orphanage to a new building in St. Louis. Inside the cabin they found a few chairs, a cot, a table, and two mattress covers, which they filled with straw and used as beds. These three young sisters had grown up in comfortable homes in the prosperous city of Lyon. As Marcella Holloway, who has written about the order's early history in America says, in this frontier setting they found "plenty of opportunity to practice the spirit of poverty of the Order's holy patron, St. Joseph."

The sisters also had two small sheds to use as a schoolroom and a kitchen. Soon they had twenty local children enrolled in a day school. Each student had to bring a stool, box, or log to sit on. The sisters sewed in the evenings to provide financial support for their work. In October 1836 two motherless girls whose father was unable to provide for them were placed in the nuns' care, and two weeks later, two more orphans were sent to them. This marked the beginning of the order's work with orphans in America. At one time the Sisters of St. Joseph ran ten orphanages in the St. Louis province. The two sisters who were trained to work with the deaf arrived in St. Louis in September 1837 and opened a school for the deaf.

In 1841 the sisters moved to a new convent in St. Louis, where they ran a boarding academy and a day school. In 1845 they opened a school for African American girls, where they taught reading, writing, arithmetic, sewing and French. Father Benedict Roux came twice a week to teach the catechism. Most of the one hundred girls enrolled in the school were free blacks, but a few were slaves whose owners wanted them to learn to read and write. Local authorities closed the school in 1846, and the following year the Missouri legislature made it illegal to educate blacks. The sisters quietly defied the law and reopened the school in the mid-1850s.

By 1857 the community had grown from the original 6 pioneers to more than 150 nuns. By this time, many members of the order were emigrants from the German states or Ireland. Over the next century and a half, the work of the Sisters of St. Joseph expanded to include many schools, hospitals, and other benevolent institutions.

A number of other religious orders also played important roles in Missouri history. Three Hungarian-German Ursuline nuns left their convent in Oedenberg in 1848 in response to a call from St. Louis Archbishop Peter Kenrick for help in educating German-speaking children in Missouri. The group was led by Mother Magdalene Stehlin, superior of the convent, who had a great interest in the American mission. At the beginning of their journey they stopped at an Ursuline convent in Landshut, Bavaria, where they raised additional support for the mission. One novice joined them there, and others promised to follow. Mother Stehlin and her two original companions were the first Hungarian residents in St. Louis. The convent in Bavaria sent six more nuns the following year. They brought nearly a thousand dollars in donations to support their work, and King Ludwig I of Bavaria contributed four thousand dollars to help build a new convent. Further donations came regularly from Bavarian Catholics over the next several years.

The Ursuline nuns were cloistered, which meant that the rules of their order prohibited them from leaving their convents. These rules had to be modified for them to fulfill their mission, so the sisters were given permission to live in parish convents and teach in parish schools. They were allowed to go out in public for the purposes of teaching school and attending church. The nuns returned to the St. Louis convent at the end of each school term. In addition to teaching children in St. Louis, the Ursulines opened thirty-six schools in rural Missouri. By the end of the century the order had 155 nuns in the St. Louis convent, including many from the small towns in Missouri where the sisters lived during the school year.

The origins of the Sisters of Our Lady of Charity of the Good Shepherd date back to seventeenth-century France. This religious order was committed to reforming delinquent young women. Mid-nineteenth-century America offered many opportunities for this special mission work. Most of the single Irish women who immigrated to St. Louis before the Civil War worked as domestic servants, but Katharine Corbett says that some who were "unable or unwilling to do domestic work drifted into prostitution." In 1849 the Sisters of the Good Shepherd founded a home in St. Louis for "the reformation of fallen women and the preservation of young girls in danger." Most of the nuns in this order were Irish, but an Italian and a German were among the first to come to St. Louis. Corbett says some women came to the convent of their own accord. Others were brought by parents or priests. Girls committed to the public juvenile reformatory for prostitution sometimes came to the convent instead. Reformed prostitutes were allowed to stay as long as they wanted, but they could not join the order because chastity was a requirement. Some, however, became nuns in a special contemplative order called the Magdalens.

The Sisters of Mercy were Irish nuns dedicated to serving the poor in their homes. As Kerry Patch grew, Jesuit Father Arnold Damen, pastor of the nearby St. Francis Xavier Church, grew alarmed by the problems in the poverty-ridden Irish neighborhood. The Sisters of Mercy was the first organization in St. Louis to provide assistance to the poor outside an institutional setting. According to Corbett, their lack of resources nearly defeated their efforts in their first years in the city. Six sisters arrived in June 1856 and began to care for the poor and sick of the neighborhood. In August they opened a free school for girls at St. Xavier's and a Sunday school for black women and girls. By the end of the year, the convent housed an orphanage, an industrial school for girls, and a free shelter for unemployed girls. The girls received a basic education and training in domestic skills and sewing. The needs of the neighborhood exceeded the order's resources. Although Father Damen had paid for their transportation to St. Louis and given them a house for a convent and two other houses to rent out, in their first years they were forced to supplement the rents with donations, proceeds from a bazaar and a raffle, and income from doing laundry and sewing in the evenings. They were "rarely much better off than the poor they served," according to Corbett. Even so, the order

Anna Gertrude Kleinsorge grew up in Westphalia and was one of many young women from Missouri who found careers as teachers or nurses in religious orders. She is shown here in 1875 as Sister Mary Heribertha, the name she took as a School Sister of Notre Dame. (A. E. Schroeder Collection, courtesy of Ed Bode)

grew, and in 1860 Archbishop Kenrick helped them find space to open St. Joseph's Convent of Mercy.

In 1858 the School Sisters of Notre Dame opened a parish school for girls at St. Joseph's Church, the largest German Catholic church in St. Louis. Corbett reports that at the end of the school year, the clergy and parents in the parish were happy with the students' academic progress but "were particularly pleased with exhibits of their sewing, darning, and crocheting skills." The churches of Sts. Peter and Paul, St. Liborius, and St. Lawrence O'Toole, all with large numbers of Irish and German parishioners, asked the sisters to open schools for them as well. In addition, although the sisters did not speak Slavic languages, they opened a parish school for Bohemian children at St. John Nepomuk, enrolling ninety children. Despite some anti-Catholic sentiment among the city's Protestants, many sent their children to Catholic schools rather than to the city's Protestant-oriented public schools. By 1860 the School Sisters of Notre Dame were educating two-thirds of all the children enrolled in Catholic schools in St. Louis.

In 1872 a group of six Franciscan nuns who were refugees of the Franco-Prussian War arrived in St. Louis. They were led by a forty-nine-year-old Bavarian, Mother Mary Odilia Berger. The group arrived during an outbreak of smallpox and immediately began caring for the sick in the city's immigrant neighborhoods. Over the next several years, the order they established, the Sisters of St. Mary, grew and expanded to include an orphanage, a home for unwed mothers, and a hospital. Thirteen sisters volunteered to help during an outbreak of yellow fever in the South in 1878. All contracted the disease, and five sisters died in Memphis. The order later expanded to other cities and built hospitals in St. Charles, Sedalia, and other Missouri towns.

Although several orders of nuns came in response to pleas from bishops, not all relations between nuns and Church authorities were cordial. Another group of Franciscan nuns, the Sisters of Mary Immaculate from Joliet, Illinois, taught immigrant children at St. Stanislaus, a church founded in 1891 to serve St. Louis's growing Polish population. The priest, Father Stanowski, complained that the order did not assign enough Polish sisters to the parish. In 1901, Mother M. Alexandra, the superior of the order, asked Archbishop John J. Kain for permission to withdraw the members of her order from the parish school. He granted her permission to withdraw but said that three of the four sisters must remain at St. Stanislaus. Mother Alexandra then commanded the three sisters to recognize her authority and return to Joliet. However, these three women— Sisters M. Solana Leczna, aged thirty-three; M. Ernestine Matz, aged twenty-eight; and M. Hilaria Matz, aged twenty—felt that God was calling them to St. Louis to begin a new religious order dedicated to the education of poor immigrant children. Over the next several months, a number of daughters of Polish immigrants asked to be admitted to the new order. The first, Sophia Kujawa, was the niece of Sister M. Solana. Another new postulant, Mary Wroblewski, had emigrated from Prussian Poland in 1892 with her parents and her sister Elizabeth. They were members of the St. Stanislaus parish. Mary had worked in a cracker factory since she was twelve to help supplement the family's income. In December 1901, when the sisters received their formal letter of approval from Archbishop Kain, the community had eight members, and two more young women from the parish joined the order the next spring. The sisters taught religion, English, and Polish language and culture, as well as other subjects. M. Angela Senyszyn, who has studied the history of Polish immigrants in St. Louis, says that "the Polish community of St. Louis took great pride in having their own sisterhood."

There were also Catholic orders in rural Missouri. In 1874 five Swiss nuns arrived at Maryville, in northwest Missouri. They had come to assist the missionary work of the Engelberg Benedictine Abbey. Linda Pickle describes their lodgings as "two small window-less rooms above a rickety rectory near the dilapidated church, a half-mile out of town." Snow drifted in through the walls and roof the first winter. The work was not quite what they had expected, either. In addition to teaching the children and attending to their own needs, "they cooked, cleaned, sewed, and washed for the priests, cleaned the church, provided the music and acted as acolytes at the

The nuns of the Benedictine convent at Clyde in 1908. The community
had grown from the five original members to nearly one hundred nuns.
The nuns founded an orphanage and girls school for both day students
and boarders. Their farm produced meat, milk, and eggs. In the 1930s the
order shifted its focus to contemplative prayer. (Courtesy of the
Benedictine Sisters of Perpetual Adoration, Clyde)

services, and even took care of the priests' horses." Not long after
their arrival, Sister Scholastic von Matt said, "I am so tired in the
evening that I don't want to either stand or kneel to pray." Pickle
notes that the nuns in northwest Missouri experienced the physical
stresses of frontier life much as women in families did. The hard
work and difficult conditions took a significant toll on individual
sisters and on the order, which suffered from factionalism and strife
during its early years.

Throughout the nineteenth century, bishops in Missouri looked
to convents in Europe for women to teach the children of Catholic

families and to care for the sick and abandoned. Many nuns responded to these calls for help. Like other immigrants, they had to adapt themselves to their new environment. Nuns on the frontier experienced many of the same physical challenges that secular women did. Nuns in some city neighborhoods were hardly better off than the poor they served. Not all of them survived the experience. Those who did made lasting contributions to the state's religious life and the well-being of its people.

Chapter 10

Women and the Civil War

☙❀❧

The Civil War brought deep divisions and great upheaval to life in Missouri. Nearly 140,000 men from Missouri—more than from any other state in the nation—fought in the war, 109,000 for the Union and 30,000 for the Confederacy. The women of Missouri, including recent immigrants, were also affected by these events. Many American-born Missouri residents, especially those living outside St. Louis, had come from slaveholding states such as Kentucky, Tennessee, Virginia, and North Carolina. Southern sympathizers were very politically influential; among them was Governor Claiborne Fox Jackson. Many other American-born residents and most of the state's considerable number of foreign-born residents were opposed to slavery and secession from the Union.

St. Louis was Missouri's Union stronghold, but families and neighbors there as elsewhere in the state were divided in their allegiances. Nearly all Germans in the city and a large portion of the Irish opposed secession. Nine of the ten regiments of Union volunteers raised in St. Louis were primarily German. William Faherty says that most of St. Louis's poor Irish were pro-Union, but neighborhood rivalries with the Germans had led some of them to join the Minutemen, a pro-southern military group, and thus they found themselves drawn into the state militia at the beginning of the war.

79

In May 1861, German Home Guard forces under Union commander Captain Nathaniel Lyon surrounded and captured the state militia at Camp Jackson. This pivotal event helped keep Missouri in the Union by eliminating the immediate military threat to the U.S. arsenal in St. Louis from the state's pro-secessionist government. Violence broke out as the captured soldiers were marched back to the arsenal through crowds of southern sympathizers, but Missouri remained firmly in the Union.

Immigrant families throughout the state were affected by the war. Elise Dubach married Christian Isely in St. Joseph in May 1861 just before her nineteenth birthday. He was thirty-three. When General Sterling Price's army approached St. Joseph, Christian and other avowed unionists fled the city. During the occupation, Elise refused an offer to take shelter with other women in a neighbor's basement, but she took a hatchet to bed with her, "determined to use it on any intruder." In October Christian enlisted in the Union army. Elise's seventeen-year-old brother, Adolph, and two of her stepbrothers also enlisted. In *Sunbonnet Days* she wrote:

> I wept when Christian told me that he felt it was his duty to enlist. In fact I cried myself to sleep every night for a year. But I wanted him to go. My only regret was that I, too, was not a man. There came into the hearts of all of us the feeling that no sacrifice would be too great for the cause. This feeling swept the entire border, inspiring the people with sacrificial spirit. All that counted was the war. Friends, family, and home were of secondary importance.

Adolph, who was in the Fifth Kansas Infantry, died in February 1862 of pneumonia caught after sleeping in sodden blankets in the snow. His regiment did not have tents. Christian, too, became desperately ill after exposure in a March blizzard. He spent six weeks in the hospital. Elise and Christian's first child was born on June 28, 1862, and they named him Adolph in memory of the brother who had died for his adopted country. The baby became ill and died when he was only four months old while Elise was living in St.

Joseph with a stepsister and her husband. She recorded how valuable her sister's company was while they nursed the sick baby together, but she left no account of how she felt when she had to bury this child while her husband was away fighting in the Union army. No doubt his absence was an added hardship.

Christian suggested Elise return to her interrupted schooling, because it would help take her mind off her grief. Elise attended a school for girls, with classmates who were both Union and Confederate sympathizers. She also attended the Presbyterian Church in St. Joseph, whose members fought on both sides of the war. Many churches split apart during this time, but Elise said the pastor of her church, Mr. Fackler, "held his mixed congregation together by the power of his personality and devotion to the church."

When Christian's three-year enlistment was over, he was discharged. Elise said that "he was so yellow from malaria and so emaciated from starvation rations that I wondered how he could walk." He soon began to recover his health, and by the following spring he was well enough to enlist again, but there was no need because the war was over.

Missouri's German immigrants often found themselves at odds with their southern-sympathizing neighbors. Sometimes immigrant families found themselves in the crossfire even when they did not take an active part in the conflict. In October 1862 Confederate guerrillas attacked the German Lutheran congregation at Concordia when the members were gathered to celebrate three baptisms. They took eleven men prisoner. The pastor's wife, Marie Wurmb Biltz, the only woman present who could speak English, begged the men not to kill her husband. The guerrillas shot most of the men, killing several, but he was spared.

Although no military action took place in St. Louis after the Camp Jackson affair, the city was under martial law from August 1861 until March 1865. Thousands of prisoners of war, wounded soldiers, and refugees were housed in the city during those years in both public buildings and private homes. The property of Confederate sympathizers who had remained in the city was sometimes seized and sold to pay for refugee relief.

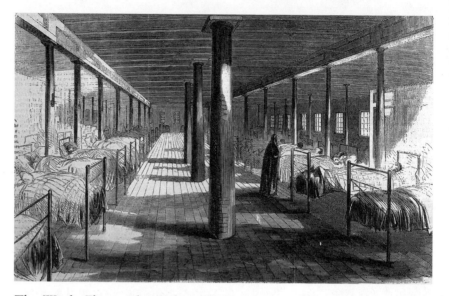

The Ward. Floating hospital on the Mississippi. Wood engraving after Theodore R. Davis from *Harper's Weekly*, May 9, 1863. (Missouri Historical Society Library)

Middle-class women in St. Louis were already involved in charitable work, but Katharine Corbett writes that during the war "women's charity became more public, more political, and more intertwined with that of men." Civilian organizations were essential in the work of caring for refugees as well as for the wounded, both soldiers and civilians. As part of this effort, a group of prominent St. Louis women founded the Ladies' Union Aid Society to provide care and comfort to wounded Union soldiers. They worked closely with the Western Sanitary Commission, the official relief agency authorized by the army and run by men. Together these two groups eventually supplied nearly fifty hospitals in Missouri and neighboring states as well as floating hospitals on the Mississippi and hospital railroad cars for transporting wounded soldiers.

Adaline Weston Couzins was active in the Ladies' Union Aid Society. She had been born in England and had immigrated to America at the age of eight. She was married to John E. D. Couzins who was St. Louis's chief of police and acting provost marshal during the war. Adaline worked as a volunteer nurse for Simon Pollak, a civilian surgeon working for the army. In 1862 the army asked the society to send volunteers to southwest Missouri battlefields to search for missing wounded. According to Corbett, Adaline and a companion "braved sub-zero weather to locate hundreds of soldiers and bring them to St. Louis hospitals." Both suffered frostbite. Pollak and Couzins were the first to use a steamboat as a floating hospital. She worked on hospital boats until the siege of Vicksburg, Mississippi, in the summer of 1863, despite the grueling nature of the work and the physical danger she was in. At Vicksburg she was shot in the knee. Even after she was injured herself, she continued to nurse the wounded until the end of the war.

The war often directly affected women's domestic lives. In many families women ran farms on their own or had to earn money for the first time. Union officers usually received regular pay, but enlisted men often went for months without wages. Their wives were left to support themselves and their children.

Mathilde Decker was a recent emigrant from Germany and only twenty-one years old when her husband, Robert, enlisted in the Union army. She had a young son, was pregnant with their second child, and had only ten dollars in cash when Robert left. For a while she moved to St. Louis County to work on a farm, but she found the work exhausting and returned to the city. Her brother gave her money to buy a sewing machine, and she was able to earn money sewing hospital garments for the Ladies' Union Aid Society. The society used this work as a way of supporting needy soldiers' wives. Mathilde sewed during the day and packed hardtack biscuits for soldiers' rations at night. In 1864 Robert came home on a medical discharge. He hovered between life and death for six months until Mathilde, against his doctor's orders, fed him a bowl of sauerkraut. He eventually recovered, and she attributed his improvement to sauerkraut's natural healing powers.

Religious orders were also affected by the war. The Ursuline nuns incurred debts during the Civil War when their income sharply decreased: school enrollment plummeted because parents were unwilling to send their daughters into a war zone. The Sisters of

Jette Bruns lost her son Heinrich in the Battle of Iuka, Mississippi. He was the first Union soldier from Jefferson City to die in battle in the Civil War. (Painting by Jerry Berneche)

Mercy regularly visited Confederate prisoners of war and civilians accused of treason at the Gratiot Street military prison. Among the civilians were some women. Sister Othelia Marshall, who was a trained nurse, and four other Daughters of Charity cared for the sick and wounded at the prison hospital.

Women's most difficult wartime hardships included fear for their loved ones and dealing with the tragedy of dead and wounded husbands, sons, fathers, brothers, and other kin. Jette Bruns's life was profoundly affected by the Civil War. Both her son Heinrich and nephew Caspar Geisberg fought in the Union army. Her son Hermann served in the Home Guard. Her husband, Bernhard, was a medical officer. In March 1862 Caspar was wounded at Fort Donelson, Tennessee. A shell smashed his left arm and damaged his leg. Three days after the battle his arm was amputated at a hospital in Mound City, Illinois. Dr. Bruns went to get him, but travel was slow, and Caspar was very weak when he got home. He suffered four days before he died. That was only the first of Jette's losses. In August 1863 she wrote to her brother:

> Our Heinrich is gone. The handsome, good boy, full of life, the pride of his father, the quiet worry and joy of his mother. He fell in battle at Iuka, Mississippi, shot through the chest. . . . And it hit us so unexpectedly, like a thunderbolt. It is too hard! Our Lord gave us the strength to suffer the first pain calmly, and so it will probably go on. But the whole war, and the whole miserable world—one gets so tired of it! . . . I almost wish that Bruns and Hermann would not be so active. I no longer have any courage for anything. I am constantly afraid.

When General Tom Price appointed Bruns assistant surgeon in the hospital in Jefferson City, Bruns found that rations were inadequate and recruited Jette and some other women to help care for the sick. Later the Sisters of Mercy from Chicago came to help. In January 1864 Bruns himself became ill, and he died in April after a great deal of suffering. Afterward, Jette said a "deadly lonesomeness" took hold of her. By the time Heinrich was killed in the war, Jette had already lost five children, three to dysentery in 1841, one infant who lived only eight days in 1847, and one to sunstroke in 1851. The deaths of her children were devastating, although many years later she wrote: "With everything that happened to me in my life, with hard trials, heavy losses, I have always found strength and courage at the right time and was never completely discouraged."

Many Missouri families experienced great personal tragedy because of the Civil War, and many women, including Jette Bruns, lived with grief and faced additional hardships long after the fighting was over. Casualties were high on both sides, and many soldiers who did return home were unable to resume their former domestic lives because of physical or mental disability.

After the war, immigration to Missouri resumed as the prospect of a better life in America once again beckoned families to forsake their homelands. Corbett says that industrialization in the decades after the war provided new opportunities for both immigrant and American-born women as consumers, workers, and social reformers, but she notes that deep divisions of race, gender, and class remained and would limit opportunity for some. In the postwar economic expansion "many families would prosper, but more would not."

Chapter 11

Immigration after the Civil War

꙰

T he new immigrants who streamed into Missouri experienced some of the same problems faced by those who had come before them. Emma Burst was a baby when her parents, Philip and Anna, decided to emigrate from a village in Alsace-Lorraine where Philip was a cabinet and furniture maker. He also made wooden toys for children. According to "Many Happy Memories and Anecdotes," an "as told to" memoir of Franceska Lutz Hennerich, Anna and Philip decided to leave France when his older brother emigrated. Emigration fever, it seems, was contagious. They chose St. Louis as their destination because Philip's sister, Cunnigunda, had already settled there.

Philip and Anna arrived in St. Louis with their four young children, Emil, Otto, Steve, and baby Emma. A new baby was born shortly after they arrived. Unfortunately, Philip, Anna, and the new baby died during a cholera outbreak in 1868, leaving the four older children orphaned. Emil, eleven, tried to keep the family together, but the children were soon placed in an orphanage. Emil went to live with an uncle who was a bricklayer. Otto was taken by a farm family in Illinois, and Steve went to a truck gardener elsewhere in the St. Louis area. Emma, less than three years old, was adopted by a well-to-do couple named Diengert. Mr. Diengert was an editor for a German-language newspaper in St. Louis. Later the

Bridget (Bertie) Byrne, from County Mayo in Ireland, in her wedding dress. She was married in St. Louis in 1887. (Courtesy of Dennis and Mary Ann Nielsen)

family moved to Cleveland, where he worked for another German paper. The children had been baptized in the Catholic Church, but Emma was raised as a Lutheran in her adopted family. Although the Burst children were separated at a young age and for a number of years the boys did not know what had become of Emma, they were fortunate to be able to keep in touch with each other throughout their lives.

Irish immigrants continued to come into the state, too. Bridget Byrne was born in County Mayo in 1869. She lived on a farm in the Knock parish and left Ireland for America when she was thirteen or fourteen. She traveled with a family friend, who had relatives living in St. Louis. First she found work in the city as a maid for the wealthy Mullanphy family. She married Andrew McCullen, a second-generation Irish American, in 1887. Bridget and Andrew lived in the Irish neighborhood of Kerry Patch. After she married, Bridget worked as a seamstress in one of the city's garment factories. She had thirteen children, four of whom died at an early age. Her husband was killed in an accident while working at the Schubert Theater. The settlement she received after the accident allowed her to leave Kerry Patch, where her boys were always getting into trouble, and buy a house in Overland, in St. Louis County.

Other new immigrants were dispersing throughout the state. In 1869 approximately 135 Swedes came to Bucklin in Linn County. They were part of a group of Lutherans who followed Pastor Olof Olsson to America to found a new religious colony where they would have more freedom in matters of worship and doctrine than they were allowed in the State Church of Sweden, according to Emory Lindquist, who has written about the group. Pastor Olsson planned to locate his new community in central Kansas. However, the group got separated because they had to cross the Atlantic on two ships. One group traveled from New York to Chicago and then on to Lindsborg, Kansas. The other group met a Swedish agent for the Hannibal and St. Joseph Railroad in Chicago who persuaded them to go to Missouri to make some money before settling in Kansas. They never made it to Kansas.

When they arrived in Bucklin in June 1869, they faced the immediate dilemma of where to live until cabins could be constructed. There were twenty-four families, with thirty-six children, and ten single men in the group. Many lived temporarily in the Methodist Church. They cooked on stoves outside the building and ate their meals together, and inside they hung curtains to give families some privacy. Bucklin's first child of Swedish parents was born in the church. By September the Swedes had decided to stay and had purchased land around Bucklin. Pastor Olsson, while disappointed that they had not joined him in Kansas, continued to support them. He sent Carl Walleen, a layman in his original party, to serve as a preacher and teacher for them.

In the 1880s, emigrants began coming to Missouri in larger numbers from southern and eastern Europe, particularly the Austro-Hungarian Empire, Italy, and Russia. In *Immigrant Women*, Maxine Schwartz Seller reminds readers that even though native-born Americans tended to lump them together, these immigrants brought distinctive cultural traditions with them. She notes: "Jewish women's lives were molded by a centuries-old legal and moral religious tradition. The parish and the village provided the focal point for the activities of the Polish woman. The energies and loyalties of the southern Italian woman were more likely to be absorbed by the close, virtually self-sufficient extended family." Furthermore, there were significant ideological, class, and regional differences within these groups.

Most new immigrants were still crowding into St. Louis's teeming neighborhoods. Recently arrived immigrants were among the poorest of the city's population. A newspaper reporter described one St. Louis boardinghouse's broken stairways and boarded-up windows. The building had two hundred rooms but housed more than five hundred residents, including over two hundred Polish immigrants. The fire department said that with its four wooden staircases it was a firetrap.

Another new immigrant, Rosa Cassettari, arrived in Missouri in 1884. Her story is chronicled in Marie Hall Ets's book *Rosa, The Life of an Italian Immigrant*. Rosa grew up in a silk-making village not far from Milan in northern Italy. She was abandoned at a hospital the night she was born in 1866 or 1867. The morning after Rosa was left at the hospital, a woman whose baby had died came to the hospital and asked if they had a baby who needed nursing. That family kept Rosa until she was about three years old and then another woman in the village, who was married but childless, agreed to take her.

When Rosa was about fourteen, her foster mother forced her to

Anna Rott was born in Hanover in 1853. She married Wilhelm Nielsen, originally from Copenhagen, in St. Louis in 1881. (Courtesy of Dennis and Mary Ann Nielsen)

marry a man named Santino. She had hoped to marry her childhood sweetheart, but she was beaten and starved for three days until she agreed to marry Santino. Her foster mother said to her: "I could not let you marry one of those boys who like you so much. They would let you have your own way. You need someone to control you. You need an older man to make you meek and save you for heaven in the end." Santino physically abused Rosa from the beginning of their marriage.

A few months after their marriage an agent came to the village to recruit men to work in the iron mines of Missouri. The company provided tickets for the men, who had to work about a year to pay for them. After working another year, they could send for their wives and families. Rosa was happy when Santino left and hoped she would never see him again. She was pregnant but did not know why—and she did not know how the baby was going to get out of her body. She asked her foster mother, who told her, "If you pray the Madonna with all your heart maybe the Madonna will make a miracle for you and let the baby come out without the doctor cutting you." Every night Rosa said *Ave Marias* and hoped that she would find the baby in bed beside her the next morning. When the baby was born, Rosa was delirious for three days. The doctor scolded her foster mother, saying the girl was too young to have a baby. It was not clear that either the mother or the baby would survive, but both did.

The baby had learned to walk by the time some of the men working in Missouri came back to the village. One of them came to speak to Rosa's foster mother: "Those men in the iron mines in Missouri need women to do the cooking and washing. Three men have sent back for their wives, and two for some girls to marry. Santino says for you to send Rosa. He sent money and the ticket." Rosa did not want to go, but her foster mother reminded her that Santino was her husband. "He has the right to command you. It would be a sin against God not to obey." Two weeks later Rosa was on her way to America, but she was not allowed to take her son with her.

The mining camp was two or three miles outside Union. It was a collection of wooden shacks in a treeless area near the mine. Rosa and Santino lived in two rooms, one "with a long table and benches and a big cook stove and some shelves with pans and things [and] behind was a little room with an iron-frame bed and straw mattress." Rosa bought food and cooked for several men, made their beds, cleaned their shacks, and washed their clothes once a week.

She walked to Union every two or three days to buy groceries and pick up mail. The first morning she was sent with a big sack to a nearby farm to buy some chickens from a farmer's wife. She was timid about going because she did not know any English, but she was told: "No use to know English for Mrs. Quigley. The farmers around here speak only German. You just make her understand, that's all." One aspect of camp life gave Rosa pleasure. "For breakfast there was white bread . . . and butter and coffee with cream and sugar and sausages and eggs besides! *Mamma mia!* Did all the poor people in America eat like kings?" She also liked the way she was treated by Americans. A Mr. Miller and his daughter Mabel ran the store and post office at Union. Rosa said they treated her "like I was as good as them." They helped her learn English, and in the winter they made her come in and dry her feet and get warm before walking back to the mining camp.

When Rosa became pregnant again, she still did not know how babies were born, even though she already had one child. Fortunately, during her pregnancy she helped deliver the baby of another miner's wife, named Domiana. Rosa did not know what to do when Domiana's baby was born, but Domiana explained how to use scissors and string to cut and tie the umbilical cord. She promised to help when it was time for Rosa's baby to be born, but the mine began to lay off men, and Domiana and her husband left for a new iron mine in Michigan. When Rosa give birth, she was alone in the mining shack. After the baby was born, she tied and cut the umbilical cord herself, and then she collapsed. Sometime later, a German neighbor woman found Rosa and the baby on the floor and ran to get Angelina, an older Sicilian woman who looked after the young women in the camp. Angelina bathed the baby and helped get them both into bed. Santino was angry when he got home because Rosa had no food prepared for him. He refused to bring her a bowl of water and some bread.

Rosa returned to Italy briefly to get her son and to collect Santino's money from a bank there. He was willing to let her go because he did not trust the men who went back to return with his savings. She had gained confidence in herself and was proud to show that she was learning to speak English. Shortly after she returned to the mining camp in Missouri, Santino used his savings to open a brothel and expected Rosa to move into the house with their two children and manage the business. She refused. She had been taught that it was a sin for a wife not to obey her husband, but even Rosa knew that her duty to obey did not extend that far. When Santino threatened to kill her, she left him. She fled with a small bundle of clothes and about twenty-five dollars she had saved, all in pennies. "I took that bag of pennies and my two children and the little bundle and I sneaked out," she said.

Gionin, a miner who had befriended Rosa, arranged for her to go to his cousin in Chicago. At first she did laundry for Italian plaster workers and scrubbed floors in a restaurant. Santino divorced her, and Rosa later married Gionin. They spent the rest of their lives in Chicago. Late in her life Rosa said: "Only one wish more I have: I'd love to go in *Italia* again before I die. Now I speak English good like an American I could go anywhere. . . . I wouldn't be afraid now— not of anybody. . . . Me, that's why I love America. That's what I learned in America: not to be afraid."

Chapter 12

Immigrant Farm Families

꙳

The availability of land attracted many immigrants to
Missouri. Some had owned land in Europe, but many had
been tenant farmers with scant hope of ever owning the
land they worked. At the end of the Civil War, there were still large
areas of undeveloped land suitable for farming in the state. Many
immigrant farm families were already settled in Missouri, but the
state government actively encouraged more immigration, and these
settlers developed new areas for farming.

Immigrant farm families, sometimes in groups, sometimes individually, settled throughout the state. Russell Gerlach notes several
examples of immigrant farm communities in his study of settlement
patterns in Missouri. A group of Polish farmers settled in Franklin
County before the Civil War and in 1866 established the communities of Krakow and Clover Bottoms. Swedish farmers settled near
St. Clair in the 1870s. A group of Portuguese farmers located near
the Gasconade River in Pulaski County and raised cattle and sheep.
Some French families who came from near the Swiss border established vineyards near Dillon.

In the late 1870s, several Austro-Hungarian families moved to
the Steelville area in Crawford County. John Zahorsky, author of
Austrian Immigration, Crawford County, says these immigrants were
attracted to the area because they heard that farms were cheap in

the Ozarks. These settlers were originally from the town of Mereny on the plains south of the Carpathian Mountains in northern Hungary, and they came to Missouri mostly from Pittsburgh and Cleveland. Two sisters, Amalia Zahorsky and Suzanna Slowensky, were among the first of these settlers. Suzanna's husband, Andrew, persuaded her father to invest in a tract of wooded land for the venture. Andrew used the timber to burn charcoal for the Midland Blast Furnace Company in Steelville. Meanwhile, Suzanna and their sons, Charlie and Will, raised chickens, hogs, and cows to provide the family with eggs, meat, and milk. Amalia and her husband, John, joined them in Crawford County at Suzanna's urging. Zahorsky reports that Amalia, in spite of being "a city girl," wanted to raise her boys on a farm because "she feared the degrading influence of city life on her children." Neither she nor her husband knew anything about farming, but they believed they could learn. In the beginning they received help from farm families already established in the area. Soon there were nearly one hundred Austro-Hungarians at Steelville. The old settlers of Crawford County welcomed the immigrants. The new arrivals, most of whom had German names such as Kiefer, Schmidt, and Heins, spoke German. They were called "Dutchmen" by their new neighbors. "They were accepted as Germans," Zahorsky says, "a stock which the early settlers considered to be equal to their own ancestry."

Of all the immigrant farm families that settled in Missouri, German-speakers were by far the largest group. Gerlach says the Germans placed a higher value on land quality than most other groups, and the areas where they initially settled generally had high-quality soil. Linda Pickle notes that the Germans tended to see land as a trust to be handed down to future generations: "Their persistence on the land and the intensity and productivity of their farming practices were part of a family strategy that often made these immigrants particularly successful."

German farms were generally more diversified than the farms of their English-speaking neighbors. Pickle believes that some of the differences in agricultural practices were due to the central role German women played in farm production. Their farms in the

Midwest tended to have a large and diversified investment in live-stock, perhaps because women were generally responsible for tending farm animals, and it allowed them to continue farm practices that yielded familiar domestic products. German farm families often raised sheep so they would have wool for stockings and other knitted items. Some grew flax to produce homespun linen clothing. Many cultivated grapes to make their own wine.

Virtually all work done by farm wives was unpaid, and the family consumed most of what was produced. Food production was crucial on a successful farm. In addition to meat, milk, and eggs, fruit and vegetables provided an important part of the diet on most immigrant farms, and women and children usually were responsible for tending the garden. They planted seeds, weeded, watered plants, harvested vegetables, and preserved food for the winter. By the late nineteenth century, women were able to can much of their produce. Pickle notes that in some ways rural women were often better-off than working-class women in city neighborhoods, who could not always have gardens or raise chickens.

In addition, according to Pickle, "on a diversified farm, a woman's income could make up a substantial proportion of the family's resources." Extra produce could be sold for cash or bartered for items in town. Women's income from butter and egg production was particularly important: "Butter and egg money bought the staples (flour, sugar, salt, coffee, calico, and the like) that the family could not produce, it paid the taxes in a lean year, and it made small improvements to the home possible." According to the 1880 agriculture census, in St. Charles County, where there were many German farms, farm women produced more than 200,000 pounds of butter, 10,100 pounds of cheese, and gathered more than 430,000 dozen eggs from their poultry. Pickle argues that women's cash earnings were probably generally more important than they or their families realized. "With hard work, good management, and luck, a woman could supplement her family's income and diet in important ways without leaving home," Pickle says.

John Buse, who grew up on a farm near St. Charles in the 1860s and 1870s, wrote an account of his German immigrant mother's workday during harvest season. She milked the cows, fed the chick-ens, and had breakfast ready at four o'clock in the morning. After breakfast, she did her housework and then went out to help in the fields. She put her baby down in the shade and helped pitch hay while John's father stacked it. She stopped occasionally to nurse the baby and then returned to work. Around nine o'clock she returned to the house to make the morning lunch and bring it to the field. Around eleven, she went home to prepare dinner. Buse reported that the men took two hours for dinner to rest the horses, but his mother got no rest. When she had washed the dishes and prepared the afternoon lunch, it was time to go back to the field. She worked there until dark and then went home to prepare supper, the fifth meal of the day. The men went to bed after supper, but her work was still not done. She could go to bed only after she had washed the supper dishes, prepared the kitchen for breakfast, and attended to the baby's needs.

Cesarine Senevey Melin, originally from Levier in France, wrote letters about her life on an Osage County farm in the 1850s, '60s and '70s. A number of French families had settled around Bonnots Mill. The letters begin in 1855. Cesarine's husband, Pierre, had taken ill and died, but she wrote that she and the children were get-ting along very well:

> My situation is not unpleasant. We have the means to live well, working of course, and we do not fear poverty now or in the future. It is possible to live well here with very little work. The land is very easy to maintain and is very fertile. I am very happy to have come here, and, at present, I like it very much. . . . We ride horses because it is a convenient and fast way to travel. There are no wild beasts to fear, only a few snakes that one can avoid easily and the weather here is very mild. One can harvest wheat, corn, flax, hemp, tobacco, potatoes, apples, peaches and cantaloupes, watermelons and all kinds of vegeta-bles that can be found in temperate climates.

The harvest in 1856 was "rather mediocre but no one suffered because of it." In 1860 she wrote that they had had a good harvest

Making apple butter at Overland, ca. 1870. The building in the background is an icehouse. (Missouri State Archives)

of wheat, corn, and oats. At that time, they had fourteen pigs, thirteen head of cattle, six horses, and other animals. She wrote: "My children continue to work hard and their prosperity is taking a good turn. We have already been able to use the land we cleared and we will continue to clear land for some time to come. We are always very happy to have come to America."

In 1871 they bought a threshing machine. Previously the wheat had been threshed on the ground by horses. "Now very few people do that," she said. The following year she noted they had 120 apple trees, planted in the last ten years, which were full-bearing.

Cesarine wrote about her family in her letters, too. Her son Casimer went west when he joined a fur-trading company. He married a French Canadian woman and settled near the Rocky Mountains, where they ran a store. Her daughter Julie and her son Felix married French neighbors and also farmed in Osage County. Her son Victor, her oldest child, married an American. They too, lived close, but Cesarine complained that she could not talk to her daughter-in-law, so she could not visit unless Victor was at home.

Cesarine said, "I believe that she is a good woman and I would love to be able to speak with her." Cesarine had been in America more than fifteen years, but she could not speak English.

The Italians who settled in Phelps County also came to Missouri seeking land to farm. In the mid-1890s New York millionaire Austin Corbin attempted to establish a cotton-farming community in the swampy Mississippi River floodplain in Chicot County, Arkansas, with the labor of poor Italian families. By January 1897 about a hundred families had reached the colony. Unfortunately, Corbin had been killed in an accident in June 1896, and much of the financial support he had promised the settlers never materialized. Mosquito-borne malaria ravaged the colony during the first year, and in one two-month period, more than one hundred people died. Some of the colonists relocated to northwestern Arkansas with the help of an Italian priest, Father Pietro Bandini, but another group chose to settle around Knobview in Phelps County, on land owned by the St. Louis and San Francisco Railroad.

Several men departed for Knobview early in 1898 and were followed by some forty families, most from northeastern Italy. The colonists paid the railroad an average of three dollars an acre and drew lots for forty-acre parcels of land. Robert Scheef, who has studied Missouri's wine-producing communities, reports that one of the early Italian settlers said the land they had purchased from the railroad was so barren that "even a crow had to carry its own lunch when flying over."

It had taken nearly all of their financial resources to buy the land, even with only fifteen dollars required for a down payment, and some of the settlers were destitute when they arrived. Some lived in boxcars or abandoned sheds at first. The railroad provided lumber, which allowed the group to build simple homes the first spring. Often two or three families lived together initially. Food was scarce, but John Sutton, a grocer in nearby St. James, allowed them to buy supplies on credit. There was already a Catholic church in St. James, which helped the new immigrants gain acceptance in the community.

In the early years some of the men worked for the railroad, cutting timber for ties and laying tracks for new lines. They were often

Processing grapes at Rosati. (A. E. Schroeder Collection, courtesy of James Memorial Library, St. James)

gone for months at a time, during which the women and children tended gardens. The new settlers also planted orchards and vineyards. According to one account, the Swiss settlers at Dillon shared Concord grape cuttings with their new Italian neighbors. By 1912 the town of Knobview, which was renamed Rosati in the 1930s in honor of St. Louis's Italian-born Bishop Joseph Rosati, had a school, a church, a railroad depot, a post office, a real estate office, a livery stable, a saloon, and two stores.

Dairy products provided a significant source of income in the community's early years. Milk and cheese were shipped to St. Louis every day on the Frisco railroad. In spite of the initial assessment that the land was barren, the upland prairie proved well-suited to growing grapes and other small fruits. In 1910 all the farms in the community produced grapes for wine. The settlers sold wine for seventy-five cents a gallon, and they also sold tomatoes, other garden vegetables, and cordwood. Tomatoes were so successful that they opened a cannery, where women were paid five cents for every bucket of tomatoes they peeled.

During Prohibition the Italians in Phelps County continued to cultivate grapes and even expanded their vineyards, unlike growers in most wine-producing regions. Women sorted grapes to be sold for fresh fruit or preserves. Then the grapes were crated and shipped in refrigerated train cars to the Welch Grape Juice Company's processing plant in Springdale, Arkansas, or to markets as far away as Denver and Chicago. Grapes became the main crop of the farming community during the Prohibition era, and according to Scheef, "their steadfastness kept viticulture alive in Missouri during the alcohol ban and provided a starting point for the reemergence of winemaking in the state after repeal."

Like all immigrants, farm families faced their share of hardships in their transition from the Old World to the New. Nevertheless, many were successful in their venture and believed it had been worth the effort and the risk. In 1871 Cesarine Melin added a postscript to a letter that read, in part, "If I dare to invite the world to leave and come to America I will do it. Here the farmer is peaceful. He lives much better than a French farmer and he is able to get land for his children much more easily."

Chapter 13

Town Life

I n the first three decades after the Civil War, Missouri's immigrant culture outside St. Louis was found primarily in German
villages and towns. Although there were emigrants from many
European countries scattered throughout the state, the Germans so
outnumbered all the rest that many small villages founded by other
groups, Poles in Franklin County, for example, or Anglo-Americans in Warren County or French in Osage County, became largely
German as new people poured in. Women who located in these
German areas faced situations different than those who lived in
ethnically mixed communities.

Those who settled in towns found fewer opportunities for
employment outside the home than did immigrant women in St.
Louis. Some young women worked on large, prosperous farms in
their own or neighboring communities or went to St. Louis to do
domestic work. Sometimes they married in the city, and sometimes
they returned home to marry within their own community.

Some women owned businesses in Missouri's towns, mostly various kinds of shops. A survey of towns in the heavily German counties of Jefferson, Franklin, and Gasconade in the 1880s showed many
woman-owned businesses. Millinery shops were the most common.
Washington and Hermann each had three; New Haven had four;
and several other towns had one. Women also owned and operated

butcher shops, bakeries, and dressmakers' shops; dry goods, hardware, grocery, and general stores; and at least one woman owned a restaurant. Some had inherited their businesses when their husbands died, as was the case with one of the more unusual businesswomen, Christina Graf. Born Christina Esslinger in Switzerland in 1820, she lived in Hermann, where her husband published a newspaper, *Hermanner Volksblatt*. She worked the ink roller on the press. When her husband left to fight for the Union in the Civil War, the press was buried in the backyard of the print shop for safety. After his death in 1870 she ran the paper until 1873, when she sold it. She repurchased it the next year, however, and continued to publish it and an English-language newspaper, the *Advertiser*, until 1880.

A more common business for women to run was a boardinghouse. Many women in cities and towns rented extra rooms to boarders, both as a means of income and as a way to provide housing for newly arrived immigrants who might be relatives, friends, or neighbors from home. Some ran larger-scale operations, however. A few owned and managed hotels; others took several boarders into their own large houses. This was the case with Elise Dubach's aunt, Christine. The Dubach boardinghouse was so popular that the family often had to set dining room chairs together to provide extra beds. Elise described what it was like in 1860:

> The prosperity of St. Joseph was reflected in Aunt Christine's boarding house. Patronage grew until twenty and finally thirty men boarded there. Aunt Christine set an excellent table and put everything on it where hungry men could help themselves as their appetites dictated. Her well-fed boarders spread the word that the best place to eat was at the Dubach's. The quantity and variety Aunt Christine served was remarkable. At every meal she had at least two kinds of meat. Even for breakfast she had either beefsteak and sausage or pork steak, and on Fridays she served fish for breakfast in addition to the two kinds of meat. Pancakes, doughnuts, fried mush, fried potatoes, and fruit and coffee completed the menu. In serving fruit or other food we did not serve it in little side dishes, but put it on the table in a big dish where each man could help

himself as often as he liked. There was always plenty. Dinner
and supper were proportionately greater than breakfast.

Running a boardinghouse required a tremendous amount of physical labor. In addition to cooking and serving the food and washing up after meals, Elise and Christine would have cleaned rooms,
laundered bed linens, tended the fires for cooking and heating, and
managed the business as well. Elise worked for her aunt for a time,
and she reported that the boarders were generally well behaved.
The Dubachs did not tolerate drinking, and that helped to keep the
house in order. However, she remembered a particularly large and
very drunk man entering the house one night and demanding a
meal. Elise, barely five feet tall, looked the man in the eye and
ordered him out. Surprisingly, he left. Later, one of the boarders,
Christian Isely, commended her for her bravery. He had never
noticed her before, she said, nor had she particularly taken note of
him. Christian apparently admired brave women, for this incident
began the relationship that led to their marriage.

Sometimes women were forced into business endeavors out of
desperation. In 1858, following the death of her younger brother,
Franz, Jette Bruns assumed the responsibility for his three teenage
children. Weighed down by the deaths of her nephew, her son, and
her husband in the war, she found herself responsible for Franz's two
surviving children along with her own remaining four. After her
husband's death, Jette learned that he had left large debts. Besides
those Bruns had incurred in Missouri, she was dumbfounded to find
that he had never repaid loans from her uncle and brother in Germany in the 1830s. It took help from her husband's brother Heinrich
in Westphalia, Missouri; a friend, Arnold Krekel, who was a U.S.
judge for the Western District of Missouri; and from her family in
Germany for her to survive and keep her family together. Settling
her husband's estate took decades, during which creditors brought
lawsuits against her. Twenty-seven years after Bruns's death, Jette
finally received the military pension due her based on her husband's service as a Union army doctor, and the money went to
repay her brother in Germany for a debt then almost sixty years old.

The Bruns home on Washington and High streets, Jefferson City, where Jette boarded German legislators in her home to support herself and her household. (From an Eduard Robyn lithograph, courtesy of Missouri Department of Natural Resources)

Jette considered several occupations to bring in money. "I wanted to give lessons in music and German, and then I can probably sell something from the garden, milk, etc.," she wrote her brother Heinrich in Germany. In addition to these activities, she used her large house across the street from the capitol as a boardinghouse, although she did not feel suited for the work. Unfortunately, she had few options. She took in many boarders who were Germans active in Missouri politics. Krekel dubbed her house the "radical corner," reflecting the brand of politics discussed there. Jette, who was herself very interested in politics, was so busy serving the men who ate in her dining room that she had little time to even listen to their conversations. True to her political ideals, she steadfastly refused to provide rooms to Democrats or former southern sympathizers, although she did accept English-speaking boarders.

Village women worked mostly in their homes and flower and vegetable gardens. Village and town life suited many of the immigrant women well. Unlike life on isolated farms, it allowed them closer and more frequent contact with neighbors and friends. A talk with a neighbor over the fence between back gardens helped prevent the loneliness that threatened so many of the immigrants cut off from their families in Europe.

Towns provided various social opportunities for women. Religious feasts and secular festivals, such as *Maifest* and *Oktoberfest,* were opportunities to bring the entire community together. Although men dominated formal organizations in the German communities, many sponsored events for entire families. In some of the early German settlements and some mixed communities, entertainment groups existed even before the Civil War. Hermann, Washington, Boonville, and Jefferson City had amateur theater groups that gave performances in German. These organizations resumed their activities after the war, and some continued until the end of the century. Women acted in these performances, helped with the backstage work, and made up an important part of the audiences.

Many towns also had musical organizations. These might be small family bands, such as the Schwaller Band in Westphalia, or community brass bands and small classical orchestras. Performances included German folk songs, marches, and the classical music of composers such as Mozart and Schubert. Hermann residents formed a brass band in the first year of the town's existence. Washington had an orchestra by the 1850s. Bethel's town band played an important role in all ceremonial occasions and was well known throughout northeastern Missouri. An eyewitness account of a band competition in 1847 described the audience's reaction to the band's performance:

> There were real band wagons in those days. The contesting
> bands, excepting the Dutch town [Bethel] musicians, rode in

red circus wagons, each drawn by six horses, wearing beaded blankets and head plumes. . . . The Bethel German Band drove in last . . . seated in a homemade linch-pin wagon with red running gear and blue body drawn by four mules in chain harness. . . . Before the first selection was half finished . . . [the Bethel band] had not only won the approval of its audience, but had all the competing members climbing from their elaborate wagons and conceding the contest.

Singing groups provided additional opportunities for people in many towns to perform and hear music. Music teachers were usually immigrants who also worked at other occupations. In Bethel, Conrad Finck, a pharmacist, gave music lessons to interested boys and girls for no charge. In Augusta, John Fuhr, a shoemaker, organized the singing society and taught music. Women played little role in these musical groups, but their lives were enriched by the entertainment they provided. Women did take part in music within homes and churches.

Probably the most popular and widespread groups throughout the German communities were the *Turnverein,* or Turners, which were primarily athletic organizations. In some towns the Turners were so prosperous that they built impressive buildings to house their activities. They sponsored many nonathletic events, including festivals, dances, plays, and concerts. After the Civil War, in addition to gymnastics classes (which included sessions for girls and women), the Washington *Turnverein* sponsored musical and drama groups that were particularly active. For a time, the drama group performed a play almost every two weeks. This regular entertainment must have done much to make life more enjoyable for those who lived in the town and on nearby farms.

In other Missouri German communities virtually all social life revolved around family and church. Beatrice Finck of Bethel wrote, "among my greatest joys is churchgoing." Church services afforded many women the opportunity to talk with other women they did not see otherwise. Because German churches seated men on one side of the church and women on the other, contact with other

Women's exercise class, Turner Hall, Washington, ca. 1890s. (Washington Historical Society)

women was easy and natural. Women also participated in weekly quilting groups and were essential to the planning and success of church picnics and other events.

Many small villages and their surrounding farms were settled entirely by people belonging to one church, usually Catholic or Lutheran. Music and celebrations centered on the life of the church and took place as part of the church's liturgical calendar. Celebrations of Christmas and Easter were often community festivals as well as family affairs, with special musical performances during the church services.

In addition to the major feasts of Christmas and Easter, people celebrated other important days in the church calendar. *Fastnacht*, the night before Lent began on Ash Wednesday, was marked by groups going door to door—children asking for sweets or men asking for the cups they carried to be filled with drinks, much in the manner of today's Halloween trick-or-treaters. During Rogation Days in the summer, the priest led the congregation around the parish, blessing farms as they went. Grand processions with much ceremony and decoration were organized for Corpus Christi, another summer feast day. St. Nicholas's Day, December 6, was a particularly important occasion. In many German communities St. Nicholas himself visited homes on the night before, giving treats to "good" children and chastising "bad" ones. Children were usually asked to repeat a prayer for the saint, and if they could not, they might be turned over to his companion, Black Peter, or the devil, carrying chains. These public celebrations involved women in the lives of their communities.

Women in ethnically mixed towns such as Boonville or St. Joseph often assimilated relatively quickly into American culture. In Missouri's more closely knit German villages, however, women helped maintain traditional ways. Women's role as the chief preservers of immigrant culture is well known, and the uniquely German character of life in many of Missouri's towns and villages is due in large measure to their efforts. They continued to speak the dialects of the regions from which they had emigrated and ensured that their children did as well. They preserved holiday traditions and prepared German foods for the daily table. Their efforts made Missouri more culturally diverse.

Chapter 14

Immigrant Neighborhoods in St. Louis

❧

M issouri's cities did not develop large, homogenous ethnic neighborhoods like the ones in New York, Chicago, or San Francisco. Instead, many small ethnic neighborhoods of various nationalities developed in close proximity to one another. The huge numbers of Germans in St. Louis, for instance, were spread over a large part of the city in this way. One result of this pattern is that most of these small neighborhoods, from St. Louis's Irish "Kerry Patch" to St. Joseph's Polish "Goosetown" have disappeared.

One of the most endearing images of immigrant life may be that of the tightly knit ethnic neighborhood, with its "national" church, architectural heritage, holiday celebrations, ethnic restaurants and shops, and "Old World" traditions. This charming picture has some truth to it, but it tells only a part of the story. Often these neighborhoods were produced as much by ethnic tensions as by ethnic unity. Today people tend to think of all immigrants from a country, Germany or Italy, for example, as being alike. In fact, when those immigrants came to Missouri in the nineteenth century, many of them did not think of themselves in that way. Many "Germans" considered themselves Westphalians or Bavarians or Rhinelanders. They were separated by religious and geographical differences. German Lutherans typically did not mix well with German Catho-

Catherine (Kate) Murphy, born in Ireland in 1832. She married Owen McCullen, another emigrant from Ireland, in Cincinnati, Ohio, before moving to St. Louis. The McCullens ran a boardinghouse and saloon at the foot of Washington Street near the levy, described by the *Missouri Democrat* in 1861 as a "low groggery." The McCullens lived in St. Louis until their deaths in the 1890s. (Courtesy of Dennis and Mary Ann Nielsen)

lics; both tended to socialize and marry within their own group. Immigrants from Tuscany or Genoa felt they had little in common with Sicilians, who did not think of themselves as Italians at all. Even language was divisive in these early immigrant communities. Westphalians did not speak the same variety of Low German as Bavarians, for example, and sometimes these differences made it virtually impossible for those from one group to understand those from another. Class differences also divided ethnic groups.

In spite of these tensions, many immigrants lived in urban neighborhoods populated for the most part by those who shared their language and cultural traditions. One of the more famous Missouri urban neighborhoods is Soulard in St. Louis. It was first settled in the 1830s when Madame Julia Soulard owned the land. There have been various names applied to parts of what is now Soulard, including Frenchtown and Bohemian Hill. It became what historians call a "stepping off" neighborhood, one in which new immigrants stayed while they established their new lives. They later moved on and were replaced by more recent arrivals. It is also typical of St. Louis's mixed ethnic neighborhoods, with several small pockets of different nationalities in close proximity. The first group of Europeans to settle the area as it became part of the growing city in the 1830s were the Irish. Mostly very poor and destined to remain that way for some time, the Irish of Soulard were quickly followed by more diverse groups of Germans. They spoke dialects based on region and class and were further separated by religion and a rigid social structure. Many of these early Germans soon moved to other areas of the city, setting the pattern of small concentrations of Germans rather than large homogenous neighborhoods. Germans continued to pour into the city over the remainder of the century, not all of them welcomed by their predecessors. The Saxon Lutherans led by Martin Stephan who arrived in the winter of 1838–1839, for example, were treated with hostility by many of the city's Germans. Only the Episcopalians of Christ Church publicly welcomed them and allowed them the use of their church for worship.

By contrast, when Czechs began to arrive in St. Louis early in the 1850s, Soulard's Germans welcomed them. Coming from Bohemia, where under Austrian rule German was the official language, many could speak German. Most of the Czechs were Catholic and worshipped at Sts. Peter and Paul, the new German church in Soulard. Most were literate and many were middle class, making them more welcome. One man, interviewed for a history of Soulard edited by Carolyn Hewes Toft, explained why some middle-class immigrants came to St. Louis from Bohemia. He said his family "had it pretty good over there," but after his father died they fell on hard times. In the classic manner of chain migration, he had an aunt already in St. Louis who advised them to come to America and said she would take care of them. He remembered that his mother had wanted to return home in the early years. "Most of them didn't like it when they came here because they didn't know the language, and [the Americans would] call them 'Honkys' [sic] and 'Polacks.'" By 1860 there were about 2,500 Czechs in St. Louis.

By 1854, Czechs had built their own national church in Soulard. The small wooden building was the beginning of the parish of St. John Nepomuk, the patron saint of Bohemia. In 1879 a Gothic church was built, only to be destroyed by the tornado of 1896. It was replaced by a second Gothic church, which formed the center of the Bohemian community for more than a half century. Czech organizations in the neighborhood made the immigrants feel more at home. Another Bohemian resident of Soulard during this time remembered that "in the summer they'd sit out on the sidewalk with their . . . beer and some pretzels. . . . Life was good at that time." During the latter half of the century, Germans continued to move out of Soulard as more Czechs arrived, and by the 1890s Slovaks and Lebanese immigrants had begun to move in, only to move out in the twentieth century as other groups arrived.

While the Czechs arriving in Soulard faced the common prejudices toward foreigners from the Americans in the city, there was employment for skilled and unskilled workers alike. Many found jobs as tailors, bakers, or carpenters, while those less skilled could find work in the flour and cotton mills or the tobacco factories. Not all of these jobs paid well. Cigar makers, many of whom were women, typically worked sixty hours a week for about seven dollars in the 1880s. However, after a number of years many of the newcomers were able to buy homes and gain some economic security.

Another famous ethnic neighborhood also chronicled by Toft is "the Hill," an Italian community in St. Louis whose history is dramatically different from Soulard. Although a few Italians were in Missouri already in the 1850s, in 1890 there were fewer than 1,300 in St. Louis, and the city still did not have an Italian district. Early in that decade, two separate areas attracted the Italians who were arriving. One was downtown, where they replaced the German, Irish, and Jewish populations; the other was the Hill. A rural area geographically isolated from the main part of the city, the Hill developed because of the need for laborers in the clay industry there. Here, too, Italians found Germans and Irish ahead of them. Hugo Schoessel remembered the coming of the new immigrants. When "the first Eye-talians came over here . . . about half a dozen men got together and rented the house. . . . The Germans who were here . . . mistreated the first [Italians]." He described his first impressions: "In the evening they had an accordion. They played music sitting out in the yard and singing, and us kids used to hang on the fence listenin' to 'em. We thought it was funny because we didn't understand it. And then after a while they sent for their friends and their brothers. . . . That's how they got started here."

Most of the early Italians in the city were young men. Only 8 percent brought wives and families with them. According to Gary Ross Mormino, author of *Immigrants on the Hill: Italian-Americans in St. Louis, 1882–1982*, there were only a handful of women living on the Hill before 1900.

The Hill grew more slowly than the downtown community, "Little Italy," which had two Italian parishes by 1900. However, by that time community institutions on the Hill were taking hold, and St. Ambrose Church was built in 1903. As Schoessel noted, many Italian immigrants came through the process of chain migration. Established family members and others in the community supported new arrivals. One resident explained: "My parents came here because I happened to have an aunt here who had a grocery store. At first, my mother and dad lived with them. At that time there were a lot of people who opened their home to immigrants from Italy. . . . For a small fee of like $15 or so per week the women would cook for them, wash their clothes, iron and everything."

As the Hill was evolving from a mining camp to a community, women were in great demand. Married men sent their wives money for the trip to St. Louis. Allessandro Ranciglio, a blacksmith who had come to America to make his fortune, had intended to return to Lombardy. Instead, he wrote to his wife, Maria, and instructed her to bring their son, Tony, and come to the Hill. "If you don't come here, I don't come back!" he said. Sometimes unmarried men went back home to find wives.

Some women came to St. Louis as "picture brides." Rather than traveling back to Italy, bachelors sent photographs of themselves home for their families to show to prospective brides. If a woman agreed to marry, arrangements were made by her family and the groom's, and she then departed for America to marry a man she had never met. Maria Imo Griffero came to the Hill as a picture bride. She was born in 1895 in a small village in Lombardy, where she attended school until she was eleven and then went to work in a silk mill, working thirteen hours a day, six days a week. When she met her future husband, she liked him even better than she had liked his picture. He was "really nice and fat and dressed like a soldier," she said.

Saying goodbye could be very difficult for these young women and their families. Angelina Coco Merlo, from another village in the same region, described her heartbroken father. "He grab me by the neck and start cry. I cry and he cry, and he say 'Angelina, Angelina, I no see you no more.' I say, 'I come over again, don't worry, Daddy. . . . I no gonna stay in America.'" Most, however, never went back.

Immigration to the Hill was a matter for the young, not the old. One of the distinctive features of the community in the early years of the twentieth century was the virtual absence of anyone over fifty. The colony was made up almost entirely of working-age adult men, wives, and children. Mormino says in a single year more than half of the women on the Hill gave birth. In 1914 there were 273 births on the Hill, but only 64 deaths.

The Hill continued to develop as a vibrant community with a distinctive Italian culture. In so doing, it was able to overcome serious divisions between the northerners from Lombardy and those from southern Italy and Sicily. The northerners saw themselves as stronger, smarter, and better looking (that is, taller and lighter skinned) than the southerners. Although the two groups lived interspersed rather than on separate streets, Lombards called Sicilians "blacks," and Sicilians called Lombards "pigeons," because they thought the Lombard dialect sounded like pigeons cooing. At first, each group developed its own organizations. There were, for example, the rival Nord Italia America Societa, which excluded Italians born south of Rome, and the Unione Siciliana Principeda Piedmonte, which was founded by Sicilians and southern Italians, but which admitted Italians from anywhere.

The Hill was an animated place. The *St. Louis Republic* reported in 1907: "During the day things are usually quiet, except at the cooperative stores, where the women are purchasing supplies for the evening meal. . . . Only the women are at home, and the children play in the streets. But after six o'clock there is a great change. Supper is over and as darkness falls upon The Hill . . . the sound of music breaks on the air."

Toft reports that on weekends, "it was common . . . for several neighbors to get together with a keg or two of beer, play their musical instruments, and play cards or bocce." In addition to these informal gatherings, many events were sponsored by St. Ambrose Church or one of the social or cultural associations, such as the Vicenzo Bellini Dramatic Club, which performed plays in Italian. There was a newspaper, *Il Pensiero,* and there were bakeries, delicatessens, and corner grocery stores. Lino Gambaro, one of Mormino's interviewees, said, "Every corner that didn't have a grocery store had a tavern." Until the 1920s, loaves of Lombard and Sicilian bread were delivered to homes in the neighborhood every day by horse and wagon, thrown onto front porches like newspapers.

Some of the immigrants spent the rest of their lives without ever leaving the Hill. Mormino says by the mid-1920s the Hill had evolved into "an ethnic community, noteworthy for its cohesion, stability, and permanence," qualities that were increasingly rare in St. Louis's immigrant neighborhoods. On the Hill, "successive generations of the same families, not successive waves of new faces, built a community." The Hill is a living reminder of the best that immigrant neighborhoods offered.

Christmas Eve at Union Market on Sixth Street in downtown St. Louis, 1893. With the availability of refrigerated railroad cars in the 1880s, the quality of such foods as fresh meat, produce, and dairy products improved significantly in urban markets like this one. (State Historical Society of Missouri, Columbia)

The women who lived in these urban ethnic neighborhoods helped preserve the old ways just as their counterparts on farms and in villages did. Soulard Market and the restaurants and groceries of the Hill attest to the importance of food in the traditions of the immigrants who settled in St. Louis. In the assimilation process, some of the immigrants' customs have become common elements in the lives of many who do not share their ethnic heritage.

Chapter 15

Women and Work in Industrializing Missouri

ᕰᕰᕰ

Missouri entered a period of rapid economic expansion after the Civil War. In St. Louis the construction of new railroad terminals and lines stimulated new economic activity, and the opening of new factories offered new job opportunities. St. Louis became a center for flour milling, meatpacking, and brewing, as well as for manufacturing furniture, hardware, chemicals, medicines, clothing, shoes, and other products. The population grew at a phenomenal rate after the war. In 1860 the population of St. Louis was just over 160,000. By 1870 it was more than 310,000. More than a third of the people who lived in the city at that time were foreign-born. Many more were the sons and daughters of immigrants. The construction of the Eads Bridge across the Mississippi River in 1874 made St. Louis an important link in the transcontinental railroad. The city continued to grow as a manufacturing center, and in 1880 the world's largest brewery and the two largest tobacco factories were in St. Louis. By the 1890s, St. Louis was the nation's fourth largest city. This growth created immense wealth for a few families, and St. Louis had what Katharine Corbett describes as a "small but steadily expanding" middle class.

Middle-class women had more housing and work options during

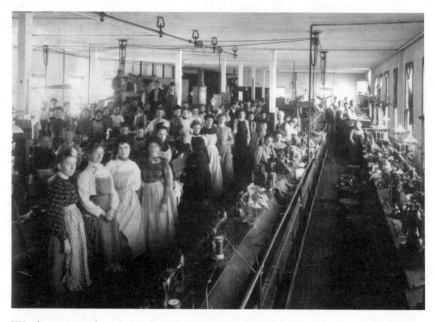

Workers at the Priesmeyer Shoe Company, Jefferson City, 1918. Although industrialization took place primarily in cities, smaller towns also had factories. Often they provided jobs for both men and women, and many of these workers were second- or third-generation members of immigrant families. (Missouri State Archives, Pat Schell Collection)

the period after the Civil War. By the 1880s, according to Corbett, many of the children of earlier German and Irish immigrants in St. Louis lived in homes with indoor plumbing and central heat. Furthermore, they could buy commercially produced food and ready-made clothing, and this reduced the amount of time they were required to spend cooking and sewing. A woman who had been a domestic worker in her youth might now be able to hire a live-in servant. Young women had new options with jobs available in offices, factories, and department stores.

Poor women saw fewer improvements in their lives. Few women earned enough to support themselves independently. Wages varied considerably, with tobacco and shoe factory workers earning considerably more than those employed in the clothing industry. Most domestic workers received room and board from their employers, and most factory workers lived at home with their parents. At the end of the century, 37 percent of St. Louis's female workers were domestic servants or laundresses, and 34 percent worked in factories. Other women worked in clerical, retail, and teaching positions. Some women were self-employed, most often as milliners or dressmakers. Few married women worked outside the home during this period, but some earned money doing laundry or piecework for clothing manufacturers in their homes. Corbett says that in all nineteenth-century American cities, between one-fourth and one-half of all working-class housewives took in boarders at any given time.

There were never enough domestic workers to meet the demand. Corbett says St. Louis employers usually preferred German girls over Irish or African Americans. Domestic workers could often save more money than other workers because they were given room and board. However, women often resented the "long hours, lack of privacy, and constant surveillance" associated with these jobs. A domestic servant had only one half-day and one evening off each week. Factory jobs in industrializing cities gave women another alternative. By 1900 many of the domestic tasks formerly done by servants had been transferred to businesses such as commercial laundries and grocery stores that delivered bread and other goods.

Female factory workers in St. Louis worked in the garment, brewing, shoe, printing, chemical, and tobacco industries. In 1890 most of the tobacco workers in St. Louis were immigrants from Germany, Bohemia, or eastern Europe. Many of the others were African American. Corbett says that women entered the tobacco factories at a young age and generally stayed until they were married. An 1890 survey of tobacco workers indicated that half had started before they were fifteen. That year the state's Bureau of Labor Statistics found children as young as nine stemming tobacco in hot, unventilated rooms. Wages ranged from two to eighteen dollars a week for the various jobs.

Twenty years later the workweek in the garment industry was fifty hours, and the standard wage was only nine dollars a week. Accidents, primarily involving fingers caught in machines, were frequent. Hannah Hennessey, who began work in a garment factory at the age of thirteen, spearheaded efforts to organize women workers in St. Louis. She worked ten hours a day, six days a week when she first went to work. She became president of Local 67, an all-female local of the United Garment Workers of America organized in 1902. She founded the St. Louis chapter of the Women's Trade Union League (WTUL) in 1907 to organize women workers to fight for workplace rights. Newly arrived Italian and Russian Jewish factory workers were recruited to join the WTUL. A twelve-year-old Russian Jewish garment worker, Anna Sandweiss, spoke about the deplorable working conditions in the factories at union fundraising meetings.

In 1909 male and female union workers at Marx and Haas Clothing, where Hanna Hennessey sewed, went on strike. Fannie Mooney Sellins, born in the United States in an Irish immigrant family, took over the leadership of Local 67 when Hannah Hennessey died of tuberculosis (the fate of many garment workers) a month after the strike began. Fannie was about forty-five years old, widowed, and the mother of three children. Fannie and an Irish coworker, Kate Hurley, went on a nationwide speaking tour to draw attention to the underpaid and overworked garment workers. They raised money to support striking workers and organized a national boycott of Marx and Haas. The strike lasted twenty-five months, but it was the boycott that finally forced the company to settle. In a 1912 strike against the Schwab Clothing Company, Fannie noted in court testimony that there were eleven nationalities among the striking workers and that their union business meetings were conducted in four or five languages.

Fannie Sellins continued her labor-organizing activities with the mineworkers in West Virginia and Pennsylvania. In 1919 she was shot from behind by hired gunmen after violence broke out on a picket line. When her killers were tried, a jury ruled that the guards had acted in self-defense. The jury denounced "the Alien and Foreign agitators who instill Anarchy and Bolshevist Doctrines into the minds of unamericans and uneducated Aliens."

The St. Louis WTUL also organized union campaigns among

women in breweries and shoe factories. They helped organize telephone operators. They initiated investigations into working conditions and lobbied for new laws to protect women workers. However, early-twentieth-century efforts to unionize working women did not dramatically improve pay or working conditions for factory workers in the city, according to Corbett. In 1915 women represented less than 5 percent of the union workers in the city.

Kansas City also became a major industrial center in the latter decades of the nineteenth century. Like St. Louis, Kansas City owed much of its growth to the building of a railroad bridge. A bridge across the Missouri River made possible the development of the city's major industry, the Kansas City Stockyards, organized in 1871 from a slaughterhouse that had opened three years earlier. At the time the city's population was about 32,000. In the next twenty years it grew to more than 132,000. By 1900 it was the largest city between St. Louis and the West Coast and one of the nation's largest banking centers.

In many ways, the neighborhood of Strawberry Hill, on the eastern edge of Kansas City, Kansas, fits our image of a successful ethnic community. In 1900 the area along the state line was populated by many new immigrants: Croats, Slovenes, Russians, Serbians, Lithuanians, Slovaks, and Poles, in addition to Germans. These groups established their own churches, businesses, and fraternal associations. Most of these immigrants, however, were poorly educted and had few skills appropriate to the new industrial cities.

Demand for workers in the stockyards that straddled the Missouri-Kansas border increased dramatically after a failed strike in 1893. Striking workers, mostly Germans and Swedes, were fired and replaced by immigrants recruited from southern and central Europe. Enticed by glowing accounts of the easy life and riches that awaited them, large numbers began to arrive in 1894. They were disdained by the Americans and hated by the older immigrants, who blamed them for helping the owners break the strike. Largely ignorant of their new country and dependent on the representatives of the industry that had recruited them, they were easily taken advantage of. At a time when unskilled workers might expect to

Work crew at the Henner and Heimes Brothers Evaporator Company, an apple-drying plant in Mayview, ca. 1910. (Missouri State Archives)

earn sixteen cents per hour, some slaughterhouse workers were paid less than four cents. Both men and women worked at the brutal jobs, even on the killing line, where they were forced to do repetitive work at a frenzied pace with dangerous tools while their feet sloshed in several inches of slippery, steaming blood. The stench was overwhelming, and injuries were frequent, even in less dangerous jobs like those in the trimming department, and workers who could not continue were simply cast off by the companies.

All family members had to contribute if there was to be any hope of success. Some of the immigrants' peasant skills were valuable in their struggle for survival. For example, many of the Croat families kept animals in their backyards. Chickens were valuable as sources of eggs and meat. Some families raised rabbits for meat, and a few even raised one or two hogs to butcher in the fall. Some Croat women went to the bottom of Strawberry Hill early in the morning to gather grain for their animals. Here trains stopped on the way to the elevators, switching cars and spilling grain. The women picked up the grain from the ground and wrapped it in large cloths that they carried home on their heads, just as they had carried bundles in the old country. Some also milked cows that had arrived overnight at the stockyards and would be slaughtered that day. Ann Bartolec remembers her mother carrying home buckets of milk from the stockyards a mile away. The women used the milk to make butter and cheese for their traditional recipes. In spite of sometimes horrendous conditions, most immigrant women survived and built successful lives, helping to develop Missouri's urban communities. They worked hard at the jobs available to them, but many also worked hard to make the lives of others better. Factory owners and others fought the attempts to bring about improvements in working conditions, and change came slowly. However, without the efforts of workers such as Hannah Hennessey and Fannie Sellins, it would never have come at all.

Chapter 16

The First Decades of the
Twentieth Century

꙳

E mma Mueller traveled to New York in the 1890s to join her
fiancé, Emil Frei. Emil had studied painting at an art academy in Munich. They were married in New York and then
moved to San Francisco, where Emil was commissioned to paint
several murals. Emma gave birth to their son, Emil Jr., in 1896.
Apparently Emma was unhappy in San Francisco, and the young
couple decided to return to Bavaria in 1898. Their journey home
took them to St. Louis, where they planned to visit friends before
continuing to New Orleans, where they would take a ship back to
Germany. Emma and Emil liked St. Louis. It seemed so German in
character that it felt like home, and they decided to stay. In 1900
the couple opened Emil Frei Art Glass Company and ran the business together until Emma retired in 1930. Emil Jr. studied art at
Washington University and joined the family firm in 1917. The
business established itself as one of the premier stained glass studios
in America and remains so today.

Until the 1920s new immigrants continued to pour into the
state. Jews were the largest new immigrant group in St. Louis in the
first decades of the twentieth century. The city's Jewish population
grew from some 10,000 to more than 50,000. Many other new
immigrants, especially from eastern and southern Europe, came

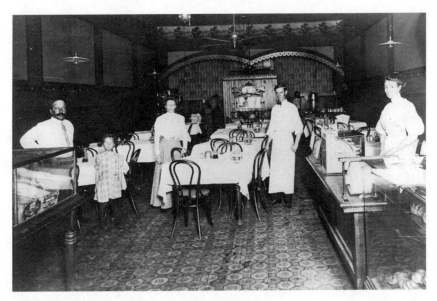

Domino's Café, an Italian immigrant business in Springfield, 1908. Left to right: Domino Danzero, his daughter Angelina, age six, his wife, Bridget, and Bertha, a waitress. In addition to the restaurant, the Danzeros later owned ravioli and macaroni factories and a wholesale grocery business. (Missouri State Archives)

during this period as well. Young women in new immigrant families often worked in St. Louis's garment industry, tobacco factories, or nut-processing plants before they married, and some women continued to work after marriage.

Immigrants continued to live in ethnic neighborhoods in the city. By 1910 there were, for example, nearly 2,800 Greeks in St. Louis. Most were young men who had come with the goal of working, saving their money, and then returning to Greece. One report from the time said there were only fifty-seven Greek women in St. Louis in 1908. Some of the men stayed, however, building successful businesses and a thriving Greek community. Some went back to Greece to find wives and then returned to St. Louis. Peter Tsichlis and a partner opened a grocery store in 1908. It prospered in the heart of St. Louis's Greektown. In 1912 Peter met and married

Margaret Delucas in the Greek village of Akrata. She was seventeen years younger than Peter, who was then about thirty-five. Most marriages at the time were arranged by families, but theirs was mutually chosen.

In the 1916 survey *The Immigrant in St. Louis,* sociologist Ruth Crawford described neighborhoods of Austrians, Hungarians and Bohemians, Italians, Poles, Jews, Russians, Spaniards, Croats, Syrians, and Rumanians. She reported that some of the worst housing conditions in the city were in the Italian and Polish neighborhoods and said this was "a standing condemnation of the indifference of landlords and the laxity of municipal authorities." Crawford's survey offers interesting insights into neighborhood life. Of the Italians in Little Italy, she said:

> The Italian women with their bright colored handkerchiefs are always found busily scrubbing or cleaning up rickety premises. Their homes are bare, and the atmosphere created by the simple fare of onions, bread and macaroni often discourages the American investigator, but one who understands, knows that numberless children, the plenitude of St. Louis soot, and the demands of industrial life, exact much of, and give little encouragement to, the Italian housekeeper in this part of town.

In addition to children, dirt, and "demands of industrial life," immigrants faced the harsh realities of urban poverty. On "Dago Hill" she said, each little home "endeavors, without success, to keep its family of small children, chickens and dogs, within bounds." The Hill had no sewers until 1914. In the Russian neighborhood women could be seen with their backs bent double, carrying heavy loads of sticks, which they had picked up near the river, presenting an image more commonly associated with peasants in Russia than with women in twentieth-century St. Louis. In the neighborhood where the Croats and Syrians lived, it was common to see a Syrian woman carrying a baby and a bundle, peddling items along the street. Often immigrants lived near major employers. For example, the Rumanian neighborhood grew up near the Liggett and Myers Tobacco Company, where many of the women worked. Crawford noted that thirty-four of the eighty-nine Catholic parishes in the city used two languages. Twenty were German and there were four Polish, three Italian, two Bohemian, two Syrian, one Croatian, one Greek, and one Slovak.

Margaret Lo Piccolo Sullivan said in *Hyphenism in St. Louis, 1900-1921* that the smallest immigrant colony in St. Louis was Hop Alley, a small Chinese neighborhood, which included restaurants, groceries, and other shops. The residents of Hop Alley were single men living communally in houses or apartments. A number of other Chinese immigrants were scattered around the city, "usually living behind their laundries." They came to Hop Alley for recreation on Sundays. According to Sullivan, there was only one Chinese woman, Mrs. Jeu Hon Yee, in St. Louis before the twentieth century.

On the other side of the state, Mexican immigrants, mostly men, began coming into Kansas City in significant numbers in the early 1900s to work on the railroads or in the meatpacking industry. Some 4,000 Bohemian, Czech, and Slovak immigrants also came to Kansas City between 1902 and 1914. Others came during this period, too, from Croatia, Greece, Sicily and other countries. By 1920, Kansas City had about 27,000 foreign-born residents.

New immigrants continued to arrive in out-state Missouri as well. They generally joined already established communities, but some formed new settlements. In 1901 the Atlas Portland Cement Company bought more than a thousand acres of land near Hannibal containing rich deposits of limestone and shale. According to Gregg Andrews, author of *City of Dust: A Cement Company Town in the Land of Tom Sawyer,* by the time the company produced its first cement in 1903 a new community had grown up around the mills and the company-owned boardinghouses. The new town, which company officials named Ilasco, was a cluster of small houses— some not much more than shacks made out of dynamite boxes— taverns, grocery stores, and other small shops.

Atlas's recruiting efforts brought many immigrants from eastern

Rosa Genovese (left) and her daughter, Daisy (front), with her father-in-law, Pasquale, and sister-in-law Josephine. This photo was taken shortly before Rosa left Italy in 1914 to join her husband, Pantaleone, in Ilasco. (Courtesy of Armenia Genovese Erlichman)

and southern Europe to Ilasco. Rumanians made up the largest immigrant group in Ilasco; Slovaks were the second largest; and a large number came from southern Italy. Smaller numbers came from Hungary, the Ukraine, Greece, and Poland. "In Ralls County, the mingling of distinctly Southern and Slavic immigrant influences produced a rich cultural tapestry and important regional variation in Missouri," Andrews says.

The cement company's labor force was predominately male, and married men often worked there for a while before sending for their wives and children. Sometimes a son who was old enough to work in the mine or the factory was sent for before the wife. Slovak Josef Hustava came to St. Louis in 1908 and took a job in a meatpacking plant. He made a couple of trips back to Europe before he persuaded his wife, Mary, who was afraid of the Atlantic crossing, to come to Missouri with their young daughter, Irene. Josef and Mary both worked in the meatpacking plant in St. Louis before they moved to Ilasco, where they worked for the cement plant. Mary sewed sacks, one of the few tasks done by women. Andrews says that in 1916 only twenty-two women were employed in Missouri's five cement plants, most of them in the bag departments.

In 1914 Italian immigrant Rosa Genovese joined her husband, Pantaleone, in Ilasco. Pantaleone had never seen their daughter, Daisy, who had been born after he left for Ilasco in 1908. They opened a grocery store while Pantaleone continued to work at the cement plant, so presumably the day-to-day operation of the store fell to Rosa. The Genoveses also took in boarders, a common way for women in Ilasco to supplement their family income.

The employees of the cement plant worked long hours for low pay in extremely dangerous working conditions. Because of the constant exposure to dust and smoke, lung-related diseases were common. Andrews notes that local newspapers often described accidents "in which victims were suffocated, burned, mutilated, and mangled by machinery, crushed by rock slides in the shale mines, blown up by premature dynamite explosions, or injured in a variety of other ways." Krajes Macra was killed when a huge beam fell on him in 1907. He left behind a wife and four children who were still in Europe. Rumanian John Moga worked as a blaster in Atlas's quarries beginning in 1903. His wife, Mary, joined him in 1906. John became a U.S. citizen in 1913 and served in the military during World War I. The couple had four children, and when John died in a quarry explosion in 1920, Mary sued Atlas for damages. The company argued that John's carelessness was to blame for the accident and fought the case. Mary's suit dragged on for nearly nine years before an out-of-court settlement was reached.

Ilasco's early residents struggled to build a community out of what was essentially a labor camp. The town's early years were "plagued by violence and crime," according to Andrews. Excessive drinking, fighting, and petty theft were common. Further, most of the early settlers in Ralls County had come to Missouri from Kentucky, Virginia, and Tennessee, and they greeted the new immigrants with Old South attitudes. Andrews says: "The disdain for Ilasco's working people that was shown by company officials, local judges and authorities, newspaper editors, and the native-born middle class was overwhelming." Living and working conditions in the town were deplorable, but the town's critics "attacked the symptoms but not the underlying causes" of its social problems. Ilasco's residents brought the customs, festivals, and religious holidays of southern and eastern Europe with them, and these too created conflict in their new society. The drinking and merrymaking that accompanied weddings and holiday celebrations typically lasted several days and disrupted the regimen of the factory workweek.

Federal legislation in the 1920s severely restricted new immigration into the United States, although immigrants continued to come in smaller numbers. Immigration did not significantly increase again until after passage of the Immigration Act of 1965, when many new immigrants began coming from Latin America, the Caribbean, and Asia.

Chapter 17

Missouri's Patchwork Quilt

❧❧❧

Immigrant women came to Missouri in the nineteenth century and still come today for many different reasons. Their experiences have varied tremendously, depending on the strength, skills, and other resources they brought with them and the conditions they found when they got here. Individual women's experiences also depended on other factors: the era in which they immigrated; their age at the time of immigration; whether they settled in a city, in a small town, on an established farm, or in a previously unsettled frontier area; whether they came as part of a family unit, with an organized group, or by themselves; and whether they settled in an ethnic enclave or a predominately Anglo-American area. Women's experiences also varied depending on what fortune or misfortune they met here.

Not all nineteenth-century immigrant women were successful. Some died before they reached their destination in the New World; some shortly after their arrival, as Elise Dubach's mother, Jeanette, did. Some died before their children grew to adulthood, as Beatrice Finck did. Some bore great sorrow as they buried their children, as Jette Bruns did. Some gave in to homesickness and grief and went home, as Luise Marbach did, and some who stayed felt that they had paid too high a price. In 1857, after more than twenty years in America but even before the deaths of her nephew, son, and hus-

Elise Dubach Isely and Christian Isely's fiftieth wedding anniversary. Elise was one of the many immigrant women who found happiness, success, and a long life in their adopted homeland. (Courtesy of John Mattox)

band in the Civil War, Jette wrote to her brother: "I have reproached myself bitterly that I did not object more strongly to move to a country to which I had never had any particular attraction and which robbed me for life of many pleasures."

On the other hand, many immigrant women survived and even thrived in Missouri. The American Dream became a reality for them. Some, as Linda Pickle documented, found contentment in their new land. Elise Dubach Isely, who "completed her Americanization" in St. Joseph as a young woman before she and her husband became pioneers on the Kansas prairie, lived to be ninety-four. In her old age she wrote with obvious contentment of keeping herself busy with sewing, attending church, and spending time with family and friends. Many immigrant women had the satisfaction of seeing their children and grandchildren grow to adulthood and become successful Americans. Immigrant and suffragette Adaline Couzins must have taken great pleasure and pride from the fact that her daughter Phoebe was the first woman to graduate from Washington University Law School. Some immigrant women had successful careers or built successful businesses, as Marie Thérèse Chouteau did by trading in land, fur, and grain in the eighteenth century; as Christine Dubach did with her St. Joseph boardinghouse in the nineteenth century; and as Emma Frei did with her husband in their stained glass firm in the twentieth century. Foreign-born women in religious orders in Missouri made significant contributions in education, health care, and other social services—work that continues to this day. One, Rose Philippine Duchesne, was canonized by the Roman Catholic Church. Remembered for her work as a pioneering missionary, she is Missouri's only official saint.

Immigrant women's efforts contributed enormously to their families' survival and success in the New World. Although much of their labor was unpaid and unacknowledged, it was indispensable nevertheless. Many women were also important as wage earners for their families at one time or another during their lives. Work that was seen as an extension of their domestic role in the home, such as doing housework for hire, or taking in washing, sewing, or boarders, was particularly common.

Immigrant women played an important role in their families' adjustment in their new home, too. In all immigrant groups, women played a key role in maintaining culture and language brought from the Old World. Pickle says that "in the home, the immigrants could preserve their old ways without coming into overt, direct conflict with the new culture around them." This was especially true in the relative isolation of the countryside, where immigrants were able to maintain their ethnic identity without the constant pressure toward assimilation that was present in the urban environment, but it was true to some extent in all areas. "The speed of a family's assimilation into American society also must have depended on the women's willingness for this to happen," according to Pickle. Women's efforts to maintain family traditions and ethnic identity helped buffer families from the trauma of being uprooted and replanted in new soil.

The Polish Falcons performing in traditional costumes at the University of Missouri–Columbia, 1980. Cultural festivals feature music, dance, food, and craft traditions that have been preserved in immigrant communities. (A. E. Schroeder Collection)

Missouri's women immigrants brought religious practices, holiday customs, and traditional foods from their homelands that have an enduring legacy in our families and communities today. Some of the customs and traditions brought to Missouri by immigrants have been lost, but others were adopted by the larger society and have become part of our lives today. Many foods brought by immigrants are now staples of the American diet. Sometimes we recognize the immigrant origin of these foods, but often we do not. We may recognize spaghetti as Italian, but we may not think of hamburgers as German. Immigrants brought many of our most familiar and widespread holiday traditions with them. "Silent Night" was written in Austria. The tradition of hanging Christmas stockings comes from the celebration of St. Nicholas's Day, a holiday celebrated in Germany and other northern European countries.

Women's experiences in Missouri's early history, with such rich variation in color and texture, created the patchwork quilt that is our heritage. The women who followed in the twentieth century added their own pieces to the quilt and helped create the Missouri we know today. The women who will come in the future will no doubt stitch in their experiences, too.

For More Reading

City of Dust: A Cement Company Town in the Land of Tom Sawyer, by Gregg Andrews (Columbia: University of Missouri Press, 2002), documents the history of Ilasco and the lives of the immigrant workers there.

Colonial Ste. Genevieve: An Adventure on the Mississippi Frontier, 2nd edition, by Carl J. Ekberg (Tucson: Patrice Press, 1996), provides a detailed portrait of life in Missouri's first settlement.

Contented among Strangers: Rural German-Speaking Women and Their Families in the Nineteenth-Century Midwest, by Linda Schelbitzke Pickle (Urbana: University of Illinois Press, 1996), examines the experiences of German immigrant women who settled on midwestern farms and in rural communities.

"Damned Plague Ships and Swimming Coffins," by Mary Cable (*American Heritage* 11, no. 5 [Aug 1960]: 74-80, 96-97), is an excellent source of information about the Atlantic crossing.

Dream by the River: Two Centuries of Saint Louis Catholicism, 1766–1997, by William B. Faherty (St. Louis: Archdiocese of Saint Louis, 1997), includes information about immigrant nuns and their role in early St. Louis.

German Settlement in Missouri: New Land, Old Ways, by Robyn Burnett and Ken Luebbering (Columbia: University of Missouri Press, 1996), gives an overview of Missouri's largest immigrant group.

Hold Dear as Always: Jette, a German Immigrant Life in Letters, edited by Adolf E. Schroeder and Carla Schulz-Geisberg (Columbia: University of Missouri Press, 1988), includes Jette Bruns's autobiography and letters describing her life in Missouri and expressing her joy, sadness, and frustration.

Immigrants on the Hill: Italian-Americans in St. Louis, 1882–1992, by Gary Ross Mormino (Columbia: University of Missouri Press, 2002), gives detailed information about the neighborhood.

In Her Place: A Guide to St. Louis Women's History, by Katharine T. Corbett (St. Louis: Missouri Historical Society Press, 1999), provides a wealth of information about women in St. Louis, including a good deal of information about immigrants.

"A Missouri Dunkard Community," by James M. Shirky (*Missouri Folklore Society Journal* 2 [1980]: 27-45), is a firsthand account of the settlement at Rockingham.

The St. Louis Irish, by William B. Faherty (St. Louis: Missouri Historical Society Press, 2001), a history of the Irish in St. Louis, includes some information about women.

Settlement Patterns in Missouri: A Study of Population Origins, by Russel Gerlach (Columbia: University of Missouri Press, 1986), is a classic study of settlement in the state.

Sunbonnet Days by Elise Dubach Isely, by Bliss Isely (Caldwell, Idaho: Caxton, 1935), is out of print, but the entire text of Elise's wonderfully detailed memoir is on the Internet at: http://home.nc. rr.com/mattoxpages/isely/sbd/

Zion on the Mississippi: The Settlement of the Saxon Lutherans in Missouri, 1839–1841, by Walter O. Forster (St. Louis: Concordia Publishing House, 1953), is a study of the settlement group lead by Pastor Martin Stephan, including information about members' experiences in St. Louis and in the Perry County settlements.

Missouri Historical Review (MHR) and *Gateway Heritage* (GH) have published a number of articles related to Missouri's immigrants. Of particular interest to readers of this work: "Prohibition Vineyards: The Italian Contribution to Viticulture in Missouri," by Robert F. Scheef (*MHR,* April 1994); "Rose Philippine Duchesne: An American Saint," by Kenneth J. Chandler (*GH,* Summer 1998); "The Sisters of St. Joseph of Carondelet," by Marcella M. Holloway (*GH,* Fall 1986); "The Swedes of Linn County, Missouri," by Emory Lindquist (*MHR*, 1951); and "Swedish Immigrant Letters in Dallas County 1837 to 1908," by C. Terence Pihlblad (*MHR*, July 1954).

Family and community histories in libraries and historical society collections can be excellent sources of information on the lives of immigrants. Notable examples include a series of pamphlets on the German colony at Bethel edited by Adolf E. Schroeder, publications on Soulard and the Hill in St. Louis edited by Carolyn Hewes Toft, and *Ethnic History of Wyandotte County* (Kansas).

The Western Historical Manuscript Collection at the University of Missouri–Columbia includes many unpublished letters, memoirs, diaries, and interviews, including Eduard Muehl's notebook, the letters of Cesarine Senevey Melin, Grant Leazenby's history of the Czech immigrants in Harrison County, and Franceska Lutz Hennerich's memoir.

Index

About the Authors

Robyn Burnett and Ken Luebbering in the mountains of western Norway, where they lived for two years while Ken was a Fulbright scholar. *Immigrant Women* was written between hikes.

Ken Luebbering was born into a Cole County farm family a century after his ancestors emigrated from Nordrhein-Westfalen to central Missouri. From 1980 to 2002 he was a professor of English at Lincoln University in Jefferson City. He was a Fulbright senior lecturer in American Studies at the University of Wroclaw in Poland in 1989–1990 and at the University of Bergen in Norway in 2002–2003 and 2003–2004. Robyn Burnett's immigrant ancestors came from the British Isles, migrating gradually from the mid-Atlantic states, through Tennessee and Illinois, their descendants eventually settling in the Missouri Ozarks. She is a freelance writer and photographer.

Burnett and Luebbering are the coauthors of two previous books: *German Settlement in Missouri: New Land, Old Ways* and *Gospels in Glass: Stained Glass Windows in Missouri Churches*.